Gardening in the City

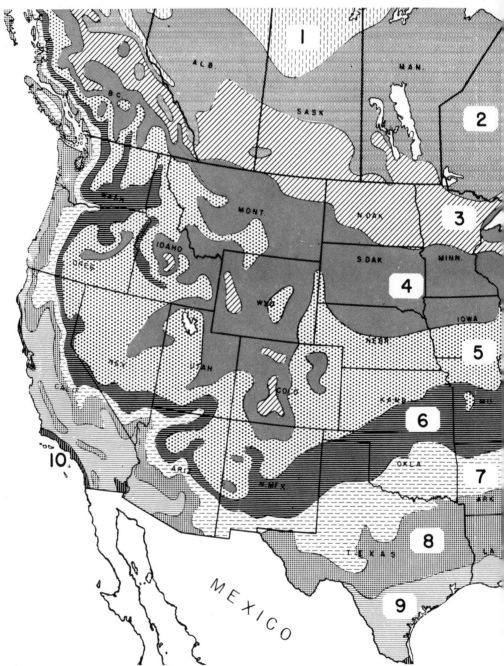

Courtesy: United States Department of Agriculture

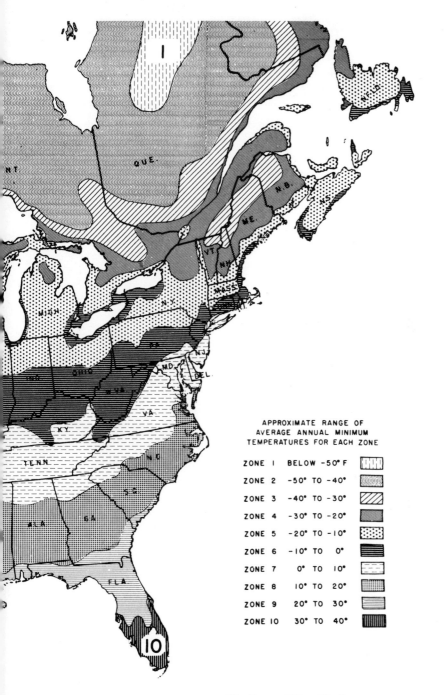

APPROXIMATE RANGE OF
AVERAGE ANNUAL MINIMUM
TEMPERATURES FOR EACH ZONE

ZONE 1	BELOW −50° F	
ZONE 2	−50° TO −40°	
ZONE 3	−40° TO −30°	
ZONE 4	−30° TO −20°	
ZONE 5	−20° TO −10°	
ZONE 6	−10° TO 0°	
ZONE 7	0° TO 10°	
ZONE 8	10° TO 20°	
ZONE 9	20° TO 30°	
ZONE 10	30° TO 40°	

The Zones of Plant Hardiness—

Gardening in the City

BACKYARDS, BALCONIES, TERRACES, AND PENTHOUSES

Carla Wallach

Harcourt Brace Jovanovich

New York and London

Printed in the United States of America

First edition

B   C   D   E

Library of Congress Cataloging in Publication Data

Wallach, Carla.
Gardening in the city.

Bibliography: p.
Includes index.
1. Gardening.   I.   Title.
SB453.W22   635.9′09173′2   76-3429
ISBN 0-15-134288-1

For my mother, an inveterate cliff dweller

I'm indebted, as I have been for all my books, to Dr. Pascal P. Pirone and Miss Elizabeth C. Hall for their help in going over the manuscript and offering valuable suggestions. Dr. Pirone, Senior Plant Pathologist, The New York Botanical Garden, and Miss Hall, Senior Librarian, The Horticultural Society of New York and Associate Curator of Education Emeritus, The New York Botanical Garden always seem to find time out of their busy lives to encourage the work of those deeply interested in horticulture. Their enthusiasm inspires the writer who in turn hopes to inspire the reader.

C.W.

Contents

Of Concern to All City Gardeners   101

Introduction

Gardening in the city. It's a little like the idea of skiing in the Sahara. Suburbanites and country people have their hands full coping with nature's frivolous whims, but when it comes to urban gardening, the challenge can intimidate the stoutest heart.

There is still a sophisticated, glamorous aura surrounding a "garden in the sky." Whether from personal recollection or from watching the late, late show, we remember movie scenes of the twenties and thirties when fabulous penthouses were synonymous with having "made it" in the big city. Strolling nonchalantly in evening clothes, champagne glass in hand, silhouetted against the breathtaking skyline, was part of a never-never land reserved for the chosen few.

Times have changed considerably since then. Today millions of apartment dwellers have terraces, even if most are no larger than the kitchen inside. Many urbanites live in townhouses with mini-sized backyard gardens. These people count their pennies just as closely as do their neighbors whose only view of the outdoors is through a windowpane.

What makes you—whether tenant or owner—pay the extra premium for access to the outdoors? The answer is simple, yet deeply rooted. It's the need to have living, growing things near you, things that you can touch, see, smell. It's the urge to dig in the soil, to watch plants grow, nurse them, rejoice when they "make it." It's the extra dimension that lounging in the sun, reading under a tree or eating alfresco brings to the confining city lifestyle.

For man, to get close to and work with nature is as essential to his survival, both emotional and physical, as are food, shelter, love. This yearning for nature can be easily satisfied in suburbia or in the country, but it's more difficult to appease in a large city.

The definition of a garden is very broad. For each person it has a different, very personal meaning. I get as much of a thrill from seeing a fire escape neatly edged with thriving plants—a key to the tenant's craving for a touch of greenery—as I do when taking a garden tour through fabulous grounds, landscaped and manicured to perfection. What matters is the pleasure each garden brings to its owner. The ingenuity, persistence, faith and optimism of the dedicated city gardener are not only to be admired but, more important, to be encouraged, because so few appear to accept the challenge. Why so many bare balconies, neglected terraces, gardens gone to weed? The interior decoration of these apartments and homes is charming—frequently very expensively done, but always lovingly. Why then this fear of tackling the design and maintenance of a tiny bit of outdoors?

In quizzing my city friends, I find that (1) they readily admit that they know next to nothing about gardening in any form. They have difficulty enough raising ordinary house plants. And (2) because of this lack of knowledge, books on gardening in general are far too advanced for them, even if they have a Ph.D., or else they can't find books geared to their special needs. They want simple, basic information, in plain language. Then, (3) some may eventually find gardening an absorbing hobby, but right now it's merely a means of getting results. And finally, (4) they are reluctant to spend money, making the outdoor area the stepchild of their overall decorating scheme simply because they don't really know how to go about it.

The purpose of this book is to help do away with these wellfounded complaints. No attempt will be made to turn cliff dwellers into enthusiastic gardeners (this is a pleasure they will discover for themselves as they go along). All they want to know is how to "furnish" that "extra room"—and because that room happens to be outdoors, they need help and guidance in doing it. The expense involved can be as little or as much as the budget allows. A good rule of thumb is to keep it in proportion to the rest of the apartment or house. Anyone who owns an expensive duplex apartment with a large terrace should not hesitate to spend proportionately when decorating the outdoors.

This brings us to fundamentals: attitude. I have had more than one client who decorated his home in a most extravagant manner, only to become highly indignant at paying a mason to do badly needed professional repairs on crumbling brick borders of flower beds. One woman insisted that her chauffeur could do the job—she owned an enormous penthouse with four exposures, a luxurious rarity in New York City. Even in the country, I have seen $200,000 homes surrounded by wastelands dotted with a few shrubs bought at bargain sales.

To obtain the maximum pleasure from his garden—whether on the ground or thirty-stories high—the city gardener must adopt the attitude that the garden is an extension of the home and needs to be furnished, maintained and given a "face-lift" from time to time just as the rest of the apartment or house does. The argument that the garden is in use only a few months of the year in some parts of the country is not valid. The same argument applies to a vacation home, and yet it too must be furnished to be enjoyed!

Apartments with terraces cost more than apartments without them. Ground-floor apartments with backyard gardens cost more than second- or third-floor apartments of brownstones. So if you're willing to pay extra for that patch of outdoors, it's because you've got certain needs that have to be met. That's a good sign, for it's the first step to successful gardening. You're already *motivated*. All you need is a bit of time, some gentle guidance and a dose of self-confidence.

A brief comment on definitions. We all know what a backyard garden is. But what's the difference between a balcony and a terrace, and a terrace and a penthouse? Simply a matter of size and location. A balcony is a very small terrace, whose floor space can hold only one or two chairs or a few tubs of plants (but there are many tricks that can be done to make such a small space attractive). A terrace is anything larger than a balcony. It can go all around the building and accommodate one-hundred guests at cocktails, or it can be what the overwhelming majority of terraces are today: a medium-sized area large enough to take a dining set and two lounge chairs plus an adequate amount of plant material. A penthouse is nothing more than a terrace that happens to be at the very top of a building. It is really a rooftop terrace. It can be tiny or larger than many suburban gardens. It can even be on several levels! Despite its luxurious connotation, a penthouse may be smaller than the terrace located on the floor below it. It all depends on the architecture of the building and the design of its setbacks.

There is no mystique to gardening, no matter *where,* you need only a little know-how teamed with some good old elbow-grease . . . so go to it!

Down-to-Earth Gardening: The City Backyard

Many houses in cities have no room for flower beds, even though they are some distance from the city center. If there is a porch, one solution is lots of window boxes filled with everblooming annuals, with perennials used as foundation plants to hide the understructure of the porch. For those houses without porches, groupings of containers near the front and back doors create colorful "gardens."
George Taloumis

The backyard garden, sometimes called a patio, takes many forms: it could be a formal garden behind an imposing townhouse, or perhaps a small lot behind a frame house found in the quieter and older sections of any city, a wistful bit of suburbia within city limits. Frequently, the garage takes up most of the lot in the rear of such an older house, leaving space for gardening only at the front and sides of the house. But what one most often thinks of as a city garden is the usually long and narrow backyard of a brownstone. Hidden behind the cold facade can be a charming retreat from city tensions, verdant and lush—or it can be little more than a neglected weed patch. It all depends on the outlook of the owner.

Planning a garden in the city demands more self-control than planning one in the country, because visual distance is so different. The entire city garden is viewed in one glance, as opposed to numerous vistas seen one at a time in the country. The Japanese excel at the fine art of landscaping within narrow boundaries, of focusing the eye on one small perfect plant or statuary to divert the attention away from unpleasant views and cramped space. We can learn much from these experts at urban landscaping.

This charming backyard is set on several levels, which gives it additional▶ interest. A sense of perspective is created by the placement of outdoor furniture in the distance, on another level. Trees, shrubs, and ground covers make up most of the plantings; bulbs add spring color.
Gottscho-Schleisner, Inc.

There are many definitions for what constitutes a garden, so do not despair if your only available space is the backstairs steps. The example above shows only a weeping willow, a couple of vines, and half a dozen potted plants, but these transform a dreary area into a bright spot of greenery. To the tenant of this house, it is very much a garden.
George Taloumis

1. ANALYZING YOUR NEEDS

A bit of mental groundwork at the beginning saves many hours of frustration later, as well as many dollars that could have been more wisely spent. There should first be an analysis of your life-style, and of the garden.

What do *you* expect from your garden? Is it to be admired rather than used? Chiefly a lovely view from the house as you look out the windows? A spot to enjoy alfresco dining? A place to entertain friends, weather willing, most weekends? A quiet retreat, away from the hustle and bustle of city life, reading a book or watching the birds? Primarily a playground for young children?

Are you going to allocate regular time to take care of the garden, or do you concede that it will be neglected in a short time (in which case it had better be designed with absolute minimum maintenance in mind)? Every day I walk past townhouses that sell for well into six figures and yet have the saddest looking front gardens. Vines meander into neighbors' doorways, weeds choke the pitiful flower beds and overgrown shrubs are in need of pruning. One can only wonder what the rear gardens look like. A few hours each weekend are all that would be needed to maintain these small gardens, but many owners don't have either the time or desire to tackle the job. Facing up realistically to what you are willing to contribute to maintenance is an important factor when designing the garden.

Are you the owner of the house, or are you renting the ground-floor garden apartment? This is obviously a vital question, because few if any tenants are willing to spend the significant sums needed today to transform a garden unless, of course, theirs is a very long-term lease. Tenant gardeners are responsible only for maintenance of the garden as it existed when they moved in, which usually means caring for perennials, pruning hedges and shrubs as needed and weeding. The addition of containers filled with annuals is a practical and low-cost way of bringing color to the garden. Repairs of such items as fences, gates, flooring and awnings may be the responsibility of the landlord and then again may not, depending entirely on the terms of the lease. "Maintenance," as can be seen, covers a good deal more than one might suppose at first glance.

2. ANALYZING THE GARDEN

After you've analyzed yourself, turn to the garden. Observe its *permanent* drawbacks, meaning fixed situations that can't be changed—such as the unsightly rear of a restaurant backing up to the garden, or a high-rise apartment building with numerous balconies looking down into your garden, giving you the well-known fishbowl complex. Knowing what you have to cope with helps when putting the plan down on paper. Trees and shrubs strategically placed can successfully hide most ground-level eyesores, while some sort of overhead screening, such as an awning and/or a dense shade tree, can shield you from the people-watchers on the upper floors.

What are other drawbacks to your garden, the ones that *can* be changed? Is the garden too dark, not enough sun getting through? Judicious pruning of trees by a professional will make the area lighter and airier. That's if you don't also have a lack of privacy to deal with, in which case heavy foliage is one way to screen out neighbors. A choice must be made in such circumstances. It depends on your priorities.

Is there a jungle look to the garden? Then overgrown shrubs or vines should be pruned back, thinned or perhaps some taken out altogether if such is indicated. Is the upkeep too demanding? A minimum-maintenance layout is the answer. Is the area too windy to be enjoyed comfortably while dining or reading? Partial overhead screening and/or fencing or an evergreen hedge help to reroute air currents. An awning with sides also gives good protection to the terrace area.

Is the garden dull-looking? Does it lack a "theme," a mood? Create a focal point with a specimen plant, fountain, statuary. Try handsome outdoor furniture with comfortable, brightly colored pillows to give a little pizzazz to the garden. Know what you want from your garden, and by your trying to achieve what is already visualized in your head, your garden will take on a note of distinction all its own. But you must first know what you're after, in order to spot it when you see it.

Arches under stairs are naturals for displaying statuary. This house in Charleston, South Carolina, has little garden space, but every corner is put to good use.

Gottscho-Schleisner, Inc.

After analyzing the permanent and temporary drawbacks of your garden, look carefully to see what its merits are. The garden may have few good points, but even if it's only one, that one can be effectively enhanced and spotlighted.

Is there an ornate wall of unusual design, dating back to the days when the art of masonry rivaled that of the famous Italian golden era? Then play it up with hanging plants, a graceful, airy vine, or a fountain which for maximum effect needs, but seldom gets, a handsome wall as a background. Do you have one magnificent tree, well-branched, in tip-top condition? Dramatize it by keeping the design of the garden simple, with no shrubs around the tree to distract the eye from it. Give the base of the tree a carpet of spring bulbs tucked into a bed of pachysandra. Hide a few spotlights in the ground cover for night lighting of the branches. The tree will take on a fairy-tale look every summer evening.

Is the terrace spacious, especially well built, with distinctive flooring? Turn it into a beautiful outdoor room. Go all out on furniture: dining table and gay umbrella, comfortable chairs and chaise longues, serving cart, side tables. Add a few tubs of colorful annuals. Such an outdoor addition to the house invites frequent entertaining of friends during the mild weather. A well-built brick barbecue can facilitate cookouts, if you have space.

You may have a fine specimen plant and not notice it because it's choked by other shrubs. Look carefully; if you have a finely shaped plant, whether deciduous or evergreen, give it air. It needs plenty of room to be shown off properly. Move it to another location, if necessary, where it can be the focal point of the garden. Give thought to its placement as you would for a fine piece of sculpture or a painting indoors. A specimen plant creates a mood in the garden, giving it that little unusual touch that makes it separate from others.

3. PLANNING THE GARDEN

You will be better able to plan a functional and attractive garden after answering these questions. A clear picture of your needs and of your garden, with its good and bad points, will develop. Careful planning will shape all these parts into a unified whole. No two gardens can—or should—be alike. The life-styles of the owners and the characteristics of the individual gardens are too numerous and varied to make feasible the recommendation of specific garden plans, but there are certain basic landscaping principles that are applicable to most situations.

If you are starting from scratch, it's wise to know, before planning your garden, what various materials needed to put a garden together are available today. The cost depends on your bank balance. Landscaping with top-quality materials and plants can run into impressive figures. Retaining walls, terraces on several levels, broad steps designed for sitting, gazebos, night lighting—all these easily run into five figures. It's not only a question of what you want, but of how much you're willing to spend on your outdoor room. There should be some sort of ratio between the cost of the house and your budget for landscaping. Obviously it's a matter of personal taste and life-style, but a $100,000 townhouse with a backyard consisting of a hodgepodge of weeds and uninteresting plants detracts from the value of the property. A major reason people buy houses rather than apartments in large cities is the garden, the feeling of having a tiny bit of nature right at one's own doorstep.

From a practical point of view, spending too much when the house is not super-expensive (*every* house is expensive today, but some are downright luxurious) is unwise, as you most likely will not get the money back if you sell, unless the buyer is also wild about the outdoors and fully appreciates what you have done with the garden. It's best to stick to a smaller budget, adding and improving as time goes on and as you similarly improve the house.

Imagination and know-how can create a charming, inexpensive garden. The costliest items are permanent structures such as fencing, flooring and overhead protection, but, as with a house in the country, new owners find more often than not that these structures are in fairly good condition and may need only to be repaired.

We strive for beauty when designing a garden, but to enjoy it to the fullest, comfort also must be considered. A dining terrace under a large, gay umbrella or an enchanting gazebo, both at the far end of the garden, may make a pretty picture, but not to the do-it-yourself hostess who has to cart the food, dishes, and so forth to and from the house. Guests feel guilty and obliged to offer assistance, which turns the garden into a traffic jam. If you plan to do quite a bit of outdoor entertaining, it's best to locate the eating area near the house, with easy access to the kitchen.

Raised flower beds are often preferred to ground-level ones for landscaping purposes, but they are also highly desirable for reasons of comfort. Elderly people with physical afflictions such as arthritis or back problems don't have to get down on their knees to cultivate flower beds. Containers are similarly "comfortable," for little physical strain is required to maintain them in tip-top shape. Minimum maintenance is not only for busy people with little time to give to their gardens, but also for those who may have the time but don't care to spend it gardening, or for those who physically are not up to standing on ladders to prune trees or hedges or to lifting heavy bags of soil conditioners. Owners of pets also find raised beds best.

At this point in your mental planning you have analyzed your life-style, what *you* want from the garden, the merits and drawbacks of the existing garden, the restrictions you have placed on the plan (such as budget, pets, children, little or no time for maintenance, age or health limits, etc.). The time has come to translate your ideas into more concrete form.

If the garden has been badly neglected, with deep cracks in the flooring, flower beds with crumbling edges, broken fences, not to mention a lack of decent plant material, your best bet is to call in a landscape designer. You will save money and much confusion in the long run. These designers work much the same way as do interior decorators. You pay them for everything retail, and they get the difference between that and wholesale prices. If drawings and much planning are involved, additional fees are in order, or a flat consultation fee is charged. But whatever the arrangement you make, major construction work requires the skill and experience of a landscape designer to coordinate all the details and have the garden come out the way you have visualized it. Each component must be viewed as part of a unified whole. A sleek contemporary wall would look out of place fencing a traditional, formal garden.

I cannot overemphasize the importance of following the designer's advice on the overall plan, and especially on selection of suitable plants. Unless horticulture is one's hobby, most city people lack knowledge of plant material, especially of those plants that can cope with urban conditions. I've had clients who insisted on buying the same plant even though it died year after year. By the time they came to me it took a great deal of persuasion, with much documentation, to prove to them that while the shrub might do well at their cousin's home in the country, no way would it make it in their town garden.

Nature plays the key role when you decorate the outdoors, unlike a room where *you* decide what you want. There is a great deal of plant material to choose from, in spite of the many urban restrictions, so that one needn't worry about monotony of design or lack of color in the garden. But it will *not* be like the garden you remember as a child in Wisconsin. I've heard this wistful comment by people who moved to New York City, wanting to know why their favorite plants couldn't be grown on a twentieth-floor terrace as they were back home. A landscape designer or local nursery is equipped to advise you on what is best for your site, and it's in your best interest to follow their suggestions.

4. WALLS AND FENCES

First, check your fences or walls. If they are in good condition or require only minor repairs, you're doing fine. If you have to replace them, however, many types are available and should be investigated. For the sake of ventilation (yours and the plants'), don't build a solid wall. If you're using brick, leave out a brick here and there to allow air to circulate inside the enclosed garden. Vines growing over the spaces in the wall take care of privacy. Walls of wood stakes also should have small spaces between the stakes so that the whole fence won't topple over in strong winds. Since a foundation about three feet deep has to be dug to ensure having a secure wall, whether of stone or wood, you can see why this is a job for a professional. He can judge whether a wood fence should be set in concrete, and how deeply. It's foolhardy to do a haphazard job yourself; in the first severe storm the fencing may come tumbling down and you will have to do the job all over again. Save yourself time and money. Have the job done right by an expert in the field who stands behind his work.

The type of wall you select depends on several factors. The style of the house is one, and the "mood" of the garden (Japanese, formal, woodland, contemporary, etc.) is another. The enclosure must be in harmony with the architecture of the house and the design of the planted areas. There are so many kinds of walls available in so many styles that only a firm specializing in fencing (or a landscape designer) can give you all the data. We've come a long way from the day when the only things available were a brick wall (although that's still one of the handsomest and sturdiest choices) and the sapling fence. Wood is worked in so many different ways that investigating what is offered locally is necessary before getting down to a final choice. Wood fences come in contemporary, traditional or rustic styles.

The wall or fence follows the boundary lines of the property. Of course nothing prevents you from having angles and curves, losing some space as you go along. But since space is usually at such a premium, it's best to fence in all your property in the usual rectangular fashion and let the flower beds and garden design supply the graceful effect of curves.

Any wall less than six feet high will allow neighbors to look right into your garden. Eight feet provides total privacy and shelter in excessively windy areas, but the higher the wall, the less air circulation will be available (the major reason for walls with open spaces). No need to add that you should be certain of local building codes and your property boundaries before having walls built. A professional firm knows about these things and will inform you about what may be forbidden in the area.

A traditional house and garden are best set off by brick or stone walls. These have a solid, substantial look that enhances the formality of such designs. They have the added advantage of durability. If well-constructed, they should last as long as the house. Minor periodic repairs will be all that is needed. Contemporary homes have a wider choice of fencing because wood, which complements modern lines so well, can be found in so many designs. Redwood is preferred because it is long-lasting and weather-resistant.

Long, narrow slats make a sleek-looking fence. They are used vertically, horizontally or in a combination of both. Sturdy support posts placed at intervals of four feet or so add to the overall design.

Hanging plants on a sturdy wall—whether of brick or some other material—are a good idea for backyards or terraces. The "vertical" garden saves space and breaks up the monotony of too much wall showing. Put annuals in the baskets; bulbs and shrubs in the floor planters.
George Taloumis

Grape stakes lose their usual rustic look when they are set inside a wood frame. This gives the fence a clean, modern line. A board fence requires imaginative handling because as a solid wall it gives one a prison-like feeling. But when built with vertical and horizontal boards forming an attractive design—perhaps topped by an open post-and-rail or lattice—a board fence is boldly striking. It's perfect for vines or espaliered trees. A louver fence is effective, but build it horizontally if privacy is desired. Again, these come in many designs and widths. If you want to make a bold statement, the basket-weave fence is ideal. The design can be flat or an open style which gives it more depth. This type of fencing is best left in natural wood, since painting it is a nightmare. When left to soften to a mellow color, the wood takes on a subdued look. This type of fencing is an attention-getter, a focal point, and should be used with discretion. A simple planting scheme goes best with a basket-weave fence which is also excellent for vines or espaliered plants; the weave supplies a grip for them as well as ventilation. Select the fence which is in the best proportion to the size of your garden.

Plastics have opened an entirely new world of fencing material. Plastic screening not only ensures privacy but has the added advantage of allowing light to shine through while filtering out bright sun. It can be used alone, but is handsomest when teamed with any of many varieties of wood panels. With redwood boards, plastic has a sleek contemporary look; with bamboo, it has a definite oriental flair. The use of wood with plastic is also good for ventilation, for open spaces in the wood panels allow air to circulate (which it can't do through the plastic). These spaces also disperse strong gusts of wind. Another plus of plastic is that lighting behind it creates fascinating shadows with plants at night. Make sure that the lights are properly located on your property. This applies to any wall or fence, but it's especially necessary if you're going to plant or install anything behind it.

Plate glass walls are effective where privacy is not a factor but shelter from wind is required. In port cities, townhouses facing the ocean have a problem. Privacy from neighbors and the street is needed on three sides, requiring conventional walls, but the side facing the water makes glass a natural choice. Tinted glass can be used to block out intense glare. Only if one has a beautiful unobstructed view is it practical to go to the expense of installing special plate glass of the shatterproof safety type. Here it's especially advisable to have professionals do the installation, for glass is tricky.

Top-quality wood, when left to season naturally, takes on a handsome, mellow, soft finish and is best left unpainted by those gardeners who prefer low maintenance. If the garden is tiny and very shady, the fence can be painted white or a soft mossy green. Light colors open up an area, making it seem larger than it is, but paint requires care. The owner must be prepared to give the fence periodic coats of paint to keep it in good condition.

Pierced concrete-block walls are attractive from both sides of the fence (making your neighbors happy) and are as durable as brick. Total privacy is obtained by planting vines along the walls to block out some of the "holes," especially those near the dining area. The open design of the blocks makes the wall handsome and also allows good air circulation.

By far the least expensive fencing material is the simple wire fence. Covered by an evergreen vine, it gives a small amount of privacy.

In summary, when building new walls around your garden, let a landscape designer handle the job if he's also doing the planting, or go directly to a firm specializing in this field. Look into the many materials and designs available and then select the one that best suits your budget and the architecture of the house. (Never mind what the neighbors have; it may not be right for you and anyway, they can't see your walls from their house except from first-story windows.) Unless you are a mason or an experienced do-it-yourself worker, don't attempt to construct walls or fencing without professional help. A proper foundation requiring much digging is important for stability against time and the elements, not to mention the expertise required to match design panels or other details. When this much of an investment is involved, don't gamble on an amateur job. With proper maintenance, it should last your lifetime—so go to the experts.

5. FLOORING

In a garden, whatever space is not taken up by plants must be paved. There should be a pleasing ratio between amounts of plants

Slate steps, unevenly cut, team well with gravel to form an effective edge to the circular bed. Island beds are a clever way to break up space and add interest. They are also perfect settings for statuary as focal points, as shown above. The use of several ground covers and shrubs make this a truly minimum-maintenance garden.

George Taloumis

and paving. If there is too much plant material with a small narrow path in its midst, one gets the feeling of a jungle, of overgrowth and neglect. All paving and few or no plants, and one might as well rent an apartment for all the feeling of outdoors that one gets from such a "garden."

If you are unhappy with the existing flooring of your garden, or if it requires extensive repairs, you should consider having a new one installed. As with walls or fences, flooring has to complement the architecture of the house and the style of the garden. A contemporary house with vertical louver redwood fencing is a handsome setting for paving of exposed-aggregate concrete blocks or for a redwood deck. If the planting design of the garden is informal (as opposed to flower beds in a geometric pattern), tree rounds embedded in gravel also would be attractive for a contemporary home. Brick and flagstone are naturals with traditional houses, and tile flooring is ideally suited to the Southwestern Spanish-styled home.

Whatever flooring material you select, it is *how* you use it that determines the mood it creates. Brick, when old and weathered and set in a conventional pattern, is very traditional in character, as are irregularly shaped flagstones. But brick cut in large blocks and set off with strips of wood take on a modern appearance, and so do flagstones when cut into squares and arranged in a symmetrical design. While generalities may be made as to which materials blend best with certain types of houses and gardens, keep an open mind. If a landscape designer assures you that the concrete paving, when finished, will look perfect with your formal house, trust him. It's *how* he puts it together that tells the final story.

Paving is a job for professionals. Proper drainage is vital (you want water to flow *away* from the house when it rains and when you're watering the plants). Construction experts will gladly show you the many designs and styles available, and their cost. By all means go and see some of their work in nearby areas if you can, or ask to look at photographs. As with choosing material for upholstery, it's sometimes hard to visualize how the small six-by-six-inch sample you're shown will look when it covers most of your backyard.

When in doubt, or if you're determined to do the job yourself, set the paving material in a bed of sand. This allows you to move

Effective use of two flooring materials (bricks and gravel) give a contemporary look to the design. Rocks, bamboo fencing, and a pergola with a vine are all handsome additions to this low-maintenance garden.
George Taloumis

it around if you're not satisfied with the results. The moment anything is set in concrete, you're stuck with it. Used bricks set in sand have an utterly charming look. Their mellow color and uneven texture make them unusually compatible with plants.

Gravel is probably the most inexpensive flooring material. It comes in different sizes and colors. A solid edging is required to keep the pebbles out of the flower beds (bricks set on their ends, one-third buried in the soil, make a good do-it-yourself edging).

The alley leading to the back door can be turned into an attractive area, and sometimes that is the only garden space a city house has. Bricks set in gravel form a neat path. Vines, shade-loving ground covers, and ferns are easy to maintain.
George Taloumis

Placing extra-thick sheets of plastic under the gravel keeps weeds from growing through, but keep the plastic well away from trees and shrubs because their roots must absorb moisture and oxygen. Play safe by staying away from the drip line of trees and shrubs (the area under the branches extending to the tip of the widest branch; roots roughly correspond to the breadth of branches). A drawback of gravel is that it's hard to keep clean when trees shed their leaves in the fall. Also, it's hard on children's knees. Gravel is frequently used in the service areas of larger gardens because of its low upkeep and moderate cost. It's also effective when used in combination with other paving materials.

Should your garden be large enough to accommodate one or more paths in the paved area, these are usually indicated by changing the design of the paving material so that the paths are different from the rest of the flooring. Example: if bricks are laid in a basket-weave pattern, make the paths in the running-bond pattern; or introduce a second paving material, such as concrete patio blocks combined with gravel paths. For a woodland garden, paths of pine-bark or redwood chips echo the naturalistic feeling. As with gravel, wood mulches are also a loose material and require an edging to prevent them from overflowing into nearby areas. Bricks and Belgian blocks make handsome edges for paths, as do strips of steel embedded in the soil when a contemporary look and a more definite line is desired. Railroad ties are great for a naturalistic effect.

When selecting nonporous paving material, it's of the utmost importance to remember that it should not be laid on top of tree roots (as with the plastic lining mentioned earlier). Water and oxygen must seep through to nourish the roots. Out to the drip line of trees and shrubs, use an attractive ground cover such as ivy or pachysandra. Paving the garden without mortar eliminates any danger of damaging plants; this may be the obvious answer when the drip line of a tree consumes half the garden!

As with the different kinds of mulches, the cost of paving materials is dependent on local sources. What may be inexpensive in one part of the country becomes very expensive in another part when transportation costs are added. If your heart is set on a particular style of costly paving, consider using it only in the dining area of the garden or on the terrace, paving the rest in a more moderately priced material. This also creates the feeling of a separate area, as an area rug does in a living room.

It's obvious that the more paving there is in a garden, the less maintenance there will be for the owners, due to less space available for planting. How much to pave is up to the individual and relates directly to analyzing your needs and life-style, as previously discussed. By having highly decorative flooring, good-looking outdoor furniture and containers of flowers and small shrubs, one hardly needs anything else—this is the ultimate in easy maintenance. But it also should be remembered that this plan is not the coolest if one lives where summers are hot and muggy. Paving material reflects more heat than do plants, and the latter not only reduce the garden temperature but *look* so cool as well. Lots of ground cover solves the problem of care more attractively than does excessive paving. Once established, ground covers shift for themselves and also help to "anchor" shrubs and trees to the ground, unifying the whole garden. Ground covers can be called "natural" paving materials and should be considered a part of flooring when designing the garden.

6. BUILT-IN PLANTERS

Planters can be at ground level or raised. If they are at ground level, they need to be separated from the paving area by an edging sufficiently high to keep the soil from overflowing when the plant is watered or cultivated. Edging can be made of many materials, as mentioned in the section on flooring. A popular choice is bricks, set flat for greater stability; if a higher edge is desired, add another layer of bricks, alternating them for a neat design. Steel strips, railroad ties, Belgian blocks and redwood strips also are suitable. Corrugated aluminum edging is not long-lasting, nor is it attractive. It bends easily if a heavy object knocks against it. But it's useful if you bury it in the soil when separation of roots is desirable, as in an herb bed, or in a ground cover to prevent it from taking over a flower bed.

Raised beds, unlike containers, allow plants to sink their roots right into the soil below, and they add a great deal architecturally to the design of the garden. Whatever construction material is selected, raised beds should relate to the flooring of the garden. If the garden is very small, it's best not to introduce another material

Long, narrow backyards can be "broken up" by a planter hung at a right-angle to a wall, jutting into the center of the garden. Bamboo fencing hides the utility area in the rear. These ideas are also good for long and narrow terraces.
George Taloumis

that might make the whole design too confusing; instead, repeat the patio paving material for the planters. Redwood goes well with almost anything, as do bricks. Railroad ties are most effective in a naturalistic garden, and so are natural rocks or fieldstones. Cut stone and concrete are for more formal-looking gardens. Raised beds with broad tops give pleasant additional seating space.

Since these beds are made to order—as are flooring and walls —they too are best built by professionals. However, they are easier to handle for the talented do-it-yourselfer than is paving or fencing.

A "dry" wall (one constructed without concrete) makes a fine planter for those who want to grow small rock plants in the cracks, but a certain amount of skill is necessary to put the fieldstones together. What may appear to be simply piling stones one on top of the other is actually a careful matching of flat stones. The base of such a planter has to be well beneath the soil surface and leaning toward the inside to prevent its toppling.

The width of planters depends on the size of the garden and the overall plan. There should be enough room from the wall to the edge of the planter for some smaller shrubs, with space left over for a ground cover or a few clumps of flowers. If plants are to be espaliered against the walls, planters can be narrower and kept at ground level. When it is desirable for a gardener to build a fairly high planter, the exposed bricks or stones are easily softened by a trailing ground cover spilling over the edge of the planter.

7. OVERHEAD PROTECTION

How much, if any, overhead protection to have depends largely on the needs and personality of the city gardener. The primary reason for protection is privacy, whether neighbors are looking down on you from their second-floor or their twentieth-floor windows. If entertaining friends is high on your priority list or if you enjoy daily alfresco dining during the summer months, protection from rain, wind and soot is mandatory. A garden with too much sun is rarely a problem in the city, but in cases where it might be, a shady spot is created by an overhead structure. Much depends on the architecture of the house, but in many cases the addition of an awning, an arbor-trellis or a permanent roof adds immeasurably to the looks of the house.

Awnings are gay and colorful, giving a summery feeling to a garden, but they must be put up in the spring and taken down in the fall where winters are severe. Wind, rain and pollution take a heavy toll on awnings, giving them a relatively short life compared with permanent structures. Awnings with side panels are useful in exceptionally windy areas, although they can make you feel either cozy or closed-in, depending on your degree of claustrophobia. Check local regulations. Awnings are sometimes barred.

For a small garden, where anything of a solid nature would be overpowering, a wood-lath roof or an arbor-trellis (sometimes called a pergola) is a good choice. Privacy is achieved by having vines twist their way up the support posts and by placing hanging baskets strategically. Unfortunately, neither of these structures offers shelter from the rain, so this should not be considered by people in rainy areas who look forward to much outdoor living.

A permanent roof with transparent plastic panels, which allow light to filter through, is both handsome and practical for a contemporary house. It comes in many styles which suit most modern homes. For the traditional detached city house, the terrace shelter can be a permanent structure, with a roof matching that of the house or with New Orleans-style wrought-iron pillars, if this is in harmony with the house's architecture.

For those fortunate enough to have tall, dense shade trees in their garden and to live in a mild climate, little overhead protection is needed, other than a large colorful umbrella.

Whatever type of overhead structure is chosen, let the experts install it. It is very much an extension of the house and should be treated as such—not only from the functional point of view, but from the architectural one as well.

8. TOOLSHEDS

Proper maintenance of a garden requires tools, which in turn require storage away from rain, cold and sight of people. If one has a garage, this is the logical place for them. The same is true of a large cellar. But if space can't be found anywhere, storage has to be located in the garden. Design your garden so that shrubs are planted in front of the shed, or screen it with a bamboo fence or a vine-covered trellis. Small sheds can be bought ready-made of wood or metal. Stick with dark green or brown, as these blend in best with surrounding plants. Obviously, locating the shed near the outdoor water outlet would be ideal, but it's not essential. What is important is to get it out of sight—unless, of course, space and budget permit building a gazebo-like structure to hold all your tools, pots, fertilizers, hose, etc.

9. THE MOMENT OF TRUTH, OR PUTTING IT ALL DOWN ON PAPER

This is the fun part: designing a garden that is strictly *yours*, unlike any other, for it's based on *your* needs and *your* preferences. It makes sense to avoid costly mistakes by figuring out everything on paper first. If mistakes are made, and they will be, let them be on paper. A plan will show you why you can't have that elaborate fountain unless you want to fall right into it as you step outside. What may appear feasible in a manufacturer's display room often is shown to be out of the question when transposed to your plan.

Buy a couple of sheets of graph paper and a pad of tracing paper. Add a pencil and an eraser and you're set. Let each square of the graph paper equal one square foot of your garden. Measure the garden exactly and draw it on the graph paper. Indicate any openings to areas outside the garden, permanent obstructions (such as garage, chimney or large pipes), entrance to the house and the exposures (north, south, east, west). Add the terrace, trees and any shrubs that please you, the water outlet and anything else that you wish to keep just where it is.

Place tracing paper over the graph paper, securing it with masking tape, and do your doodling on the transparent sheet. The exact dimensions of your garden will show through the paper and you'll be able to work out details: how wide your planters can be;

whether you've room for island beds and if so, whether free-form, square or round would look best. Start with what you most want from your garden: is it a place to eat, to sunbathe, to read? You've already analyzed your needs, so these answers should come quickly. Make a note to plant flowers in the part of the garden that gets the most sun and to place your favorite lounge chair in that area if you're a sun worshipper.

Avoid planting in straight lines along the walls if you can help it. Gentle curves are so much more pleasant to the eye. A path is also more inviting if it meanders diagonally from one corner of the garden to the other. Scale is vitally important, so overdoing anything is to be avoided at all cost. Too many abrupt curves, too many island beds, too many separate areas not related to one another would make for a dizzying plan. Simplicity is the keynote when designing small areas. If space is at a real premium, leave the center of the garden open and paved, planting in an irregular line all around it. Or plant only on one side (the sunny one) and have the path and lounging area on the other side.

Planting slightly smaller plants in the rear of the garden fools the eye with a "perspective," giving the garden a greater depth than it really has. This trick must be handled very subtly, however, and works best when shrubs dominate the planting scheme on either side of the garden. As the shrubs graduate in size ever so slightly, the eye becomes aware of distance.

If the garden is very long and narrow, break the tunnel-like look by introducing a second area which creates interest and gives the appearance of spaciousness. This can be done with any garden of sufficiently large proportions. A free-form border jutting into the center of the garden from one of the side walls creates a natural partition, too low to fence in the place, yet definitive enough to form a separate area. Use this second area as a reading nook furnished with comfortable chairs, as a sandbox playground for small children or as the barbecue center.

As you continue doodling on the tracing paper, consider a focal point in the garden. As with the decoration of a room, a dramatic accent to which the eye is automatically drawn gives personality to the decor. You may already have a choice specimen plant in your garden that could be highlighted. An exceptionally handsome shrub needs only sufficient space around it to capture attention. Add a carpet of ground cover at the base, or an attractive mulching of wood chips. Treat the specimen plant as you would a statue. Avoid planting anything close to it that is similar in height; keep everything low and horizontal.

A fountain against a well-constructed wall makes a superb focal point. So do garden pools, which come in all shapes and sizes and which use recirculating water. Sink the pool into the soil at surface level. For a naturalistic effect, place a few Featherocks or fiber glass rocks (these look like the real thing but weigh next to nothing) along one side, adding appropriate small plants on the other side of the pool. Simple stone statuary goes well with a garden pool. If the sculpture is important-looking, it can be the focal point all by itself, with no need for a pool.

Any container plant can be the center of attraction if it's a fine specimen in a well-designed container. A lantana or geranium standard (grown to a single stem like a tree) draws much-deserved praise, as do fuchsia and rose standards.

Take a good look at the foundation planting of your house on the side that faces the garden. Perhaps there are no plants if the paved terrace starts right at the building line, but if there are, it's a good design to relate the planting material of the garden to that by the house foundation. Repeating one or two plants in both areas increases the feeling of spaciousness and harmony, since the two areas are treated as one large space.

Because of the small size of the typical city garden, the viewer takes in the entire area in one glance, making self-control imperative in keeping the design simple. A cluttered look results from too many focal points, too many gadgets, too much furniture, too many clashing flower beds—in short, too much of anything. One important flower bed filled with masses of a few species of flowers (don't try one of everything) is vastly more impressive than two or three tiny planters scattered here and there.

Drawing a plan of the garden to scale is important in avoiding the trauma of discovering that the furniture you ordered takes up half the garden or that the pool is so tiny that it looks like a puddle after a shower. When the planters are drawn in, together with existing trees, the plan may show that there isn't space for a fountain smack in the middle of the garden if you still want room to walk around. The boundaries of the garden, with its permanent plants and structures, show clearly through the tracing paper as you sketch in your ideas, and they remind you of what's left to play around with.

Don't despair if your ground is not level. This gives the landscaping of your garden an intriguing quality. Consider a low retaining wall or broad steps (which can be used for sitting). These automatically create two areas on separate levels.

If minimum maintenance gets top priority in your plan, it doesn't mean that the garden has to be dull and monotonous. Trees, shrubs and ground covers come in so many varieties that it's easy to create an attractive effect. Combine evergreen shrubs with flowering ones, for contrast and also to avoid a totally bare look during the winter. Add ground covers to unify the shrubs and trees and to give a lush green look to the garden. Once established, ground covers require no care. Choose shrubs that won't grow beyond the size you want, in order to avoid time-consuming pruning. For a dash of color, group half a dozen or more containers filled with annuals that will bloom all summer long. Place these near the terrace area so that you can enjoy the flowers close up. Container gardening eliminates weeding. Invest in several handsome, large containers and simply put pots of flowers inside them, adding a layer of pine-bark mulch to hide the pots. If one plant dies, pull it out of the container and replace it with another. By grouping the containers together in one part of the garden instead of scattering them around, you will create an impressive, massive show of color. Use a good-looking piece of statuary as a focal point (as opposed to a specimen plant, which requires care). Show off well-built flooring with gay outdoor furniture. Planting certain varieties of bulbs in the ground cover is a once-only job that is well worth the initial effort, for daffodils and crocuses give a lift to the spirit of early spring. About the only maintenance required in such a garden is watering.

If yours is a detached house, don't overlook possible space in alleyways that separate one house from another. Sometimes the width isn't much more than three feet, but flowers or vegetables can grow if there is enough sun. If there isn't, there are still many shade-loving plants that can.

Gardens in front of the house (facing the street) are best kept simple, relying on permanent plantings unless a dedicated gardener is the owner. Better to show the world an unpretentious garden, neat, well-kept and weed-free, than an elaborate one that looks sadly neglected. Save your energy for the maintenance of the back-yard garden, where you and your family and friends can enjoy the fruits of your labor in privacy. "One-upmanship" as the motivating factor in designing front gardens gives little satisfaction and fewer rewards. Do away with overgrown shrubs and tall evergreens that block out light and sun inside the house. Compact shrubs with a ground-cover base are the easiest way to cover the foundation of a house. Avoid anything that grows past window height.

When your final garden plan is drawn on the graph paper, it should include, or you should have considered, the following items:

Walls, fencing
Flooring
Overhead protection
Built-in planters and/or containers
Existing trees and/or shrubs to be kept
Ornaments: statuary, pools, fountains, benches, birdbaths, etc.
Garden furniture for meals, lounging, entertaining
Toolshed, water faucet, drain outlets
Play area for small children

Your list of plant material will be based on the space allocated after all the essentials have been put down on paper. The larger the garden and the greater the importance you place on plants, the more of these you will need, but don't overplant. Wait a while. One or two small trees with airy foliage are plenty. You won't create any more shade than might already exist. Chances are that at least one large shade tree is already on your property, or on your neighbor's side shading your garden as well. Select shrubs not only for their beauty but also for screening unpleasant views and for greenery in winter (evergreens are tops here), or for flowers during spring and summer with brilliant fall color and bright berries. Some shrubs add little more to the landscape than green leaves; if others also have flowers and berries, why not choose these super-performers? Obviously not all will be suitable for a city garden with its many drawbacks, but there are a few shrubs that survive very well under urban conditions.

A word of caution regarding annuals and perennials: you can expect maximum blooming in the country and on terraces, but not in the average city backyard, which is usually excessively shady. It's best to be warned in advance. However, there are shade-loving flowers which will give you enough color in the garden. Plant the ones needing sun in containers which you can place in the sunniest spot of the backyard. Perennials are not nearly as free-blooming as annuals, and it takes the most careful planting of many kinds of perennials (requiring a fairly large area) to assure continuous bloom from spring through late fall. Even in the country, annuals have to come to the rescue of the perennial garden when a steady supply of flowers is desired. To keep many perennials in condition and to ensure yearly maximum bloom, they have to be dug up, divided and replanted. This may delight friends who are the happy recipients of your extra plant dividends, but it does mean work for you.

"Island" flower beds may be your solution to the shade problem if the center of the garden is open to the sky, receiving full sun while the sides of the garden are in the shade. One or more openings in the paving can make room for flower beds; this looks very dramatic. If you do this, keep in mind that such beds are viewed from all angles, so plant taller flowers in the center of the bed and circle them with lower ones as edging. If space permits, a flower bed which juts out at right angles from the wall—a little like a peninsula—is another idea for catching maximum sun. This and the island beds are the best locations for roses to grow happily— unless of course your entire backyard is bathed in sunshine, a rare occurrence in the heart of a big city. However, not every city gardener lives in the shadow of skyscrapers, so it's possible for many to grow flowers. Driving through the less densely populated parts of cities, one sees a profusion of flowers during the summer, lovingly tended by their owners. Plenty of sun is the answer.

Experienced, dedicated gardeners expect and tolerate with grace the length of time it takes plants to flower and to grow to their full size. Other gardeners are impatient, wanting instant gratification. This is especially true of urban dwellers. Their gardening is limited, so understandably it must produce results quickly. The pace of city life is so hectic that little time is available for most people to spend on the cultivation of their garden. (A great pity!) For these reasons, city gardeners resort to as many shortcuts as possible.

Buy already established plants rather than attempting to grow them from seed. If perennials are not easily available from your local garden center, there are excellent mail-order houses that specialize in them; the plants are guaranteed to arrive in excellent condition at the appropriate time for planting. Annuals are easy to buy locally and should be already blooming, if possible. This prevents clashing of colors later if they are purchased on guesswork alone. So many hybrids are being developed today that flowers come in colors that didn't exist two years ago! In large areas a multitude of colors is not jarring to the eye, but in a small backyard, forethought must be given so that they complement one another.

Another advantage of buying grown plants is that you get an indication of their growth habits. It's hard to visualize whether a tiny seedling will grow to be a squat bushy plant or a tall skinny one. Beginners are bewildered when faced with having to figure how many plants to buy in order to fill a particular planter. It's easier to do this if the plants are already sufficiently grown to give a good indication of their future size. Read the labels that come with plants, for they indicate the height of the plant at maturity.

Urban growing conditions not being as ideal as they are in the country, the city gardener can be forgiven if he plants his annuals a bit closer together than he should. He'll be sure not to get a spotty look this way, and the experience of how it turns out will teach him how many to order the following year. Keep a notebook with all sorts of bits of information gathered at the end of each summer—which plants did best, what looked terrific teamed with what other plant, and so forth. These notes will be invaluable come the following spring when you start planning and buying anew.

Perennials need room to grow, however, since they're to be in the same spot for a number of years. So it's best to give them lots of room. In the meantime, the empty spaces between them can be filled easily by annuals. It's a good idea to combine them anyway, since the blooming time of most perennials is short.

So little plant material is necessary for a city garden that it's wise to buy the best quality of trees and shrubs and as mature a plant as the budget allows. The older the plant, the bigger it is and the more it costs, but the quicker you start to enjoy it. It's discouraging, when all you have is one tree on the property, to wait ten years for it to look like anything—or to wait for shrubs to fill out and begin to make a garden look green. Buying tiny specimens may be tempting when you look at the price tag, but only gardeners with tremendous patience and a long-range view should give in to that urge. Another very good reason for buying mature plants is that you see what you're getting. Plants are very much like people. Two may have the same parents, but one will be much fuller at age three than the other. Branching habits differ and only time can bring this out. A stroll through a large nursery shows dramatically how vastly different grown plants of the same variety can look.

Make a list of the plants you need and attach it to the graph paper with the garden plan. Plant material should include the following:

> At least one tree for shade; if the garden is already shady, one small tree for beauty and to "frame" the garden
> Shrubs as background for flower beds and to make the garden green and lush-looking
> Perennials—a few clumps, plus bulbs
> Annuals—as many as space permits
> Vines for garden walls, back of house or the awning posts
> Ground cover—the "carpet" that ties everything together

Check the charts on pages 87–99 for those plants that best suit your needs and preferences. Exposure (north, south, east, west) and climate are the critical factors, since they define the amount and intensity of the sun. Also important in making selections is the function of the plant. For example, if there's room for only one tree, as a matter of personal taste some gardeners prefer an evergreen to a deciduous one (the kind that sheds its leaves in the fall). And if the tree is supposed to screen out an unpleasant view, the evergreen is most definitely the correct choice, as it will be on the job all year-around and is denser in foliage than deciduous trees. If shade is required, then evergreens are out of the question and a deciduous tree is the proper choice. When space is severely limited, a flowering fruit tree or a beautiful dogwood is a logical choice. Always ask yourself what the tree is supposed to do for the garden before making your selection. There is more involved than looks; function is also a determining factor.

10. ABOUT HOUSE PLANTS

Most house plants greatly benefit by a summer outdoors, except those huge specimen trees that are far too heavy to move and too costly an investment to gamble with by exposure to the elements. The instinct is to plunge these house plants right into the soil wherever there are empty spaces in the garden. This, however, totally ruins the appearance of a carefully planned garden. It makes for a spotty look and nobody really wins; the house plants are not shown off to best advantage and the surrounding annuals or perennials lose their massive impact.

When displaying plants, the same principle holds true outdoors that does indoors: group them together. A corner of the terrace is a natural place for them, as they can be viewed up close. Place smaller pots inside a large container to prevent the soil from drying out too quickly and to keep them from falling over in a stiff wind. A wrought-iron table or a tiered-stand provides an attractive way to display house plants and also makes caring for them that much easier. In the rare event that you grow only one type of house plant—such as a dozen wax begonias—these can be part of the regular flower bed, since there would be enough of the same variety to make a "statement." Six pink and six white begonias, mixed and planted close together, would add an attractive touch to a shady corner of the backyard. The one-of-a-kind plant collection should be grouped together and kept separate from the regular garden. Hanging baskets are beautiful hung from a pergola, from decorative hooks on the garden walls or from the lower limbs of a large tree.

11. THE ALL-IMPORTANT SOIL

Before getting down to the actual planting, let's discuss soil condition, because the success of your planting depends enormously on it. No matter how healthy and vigorous the plants you've bought and how carefully you've planted them, if the soil is poor they just won't make it. Since one seldom starts a garden from scratch, have a good look at your existing plant material. It should give a clue to the condition of the soil. Lack of luster in the leaves, twiggy or dead branches, stunted growth, dying shrubs? Even a beginner knows whether he's looking at a healthy plant or a sick one.

Most city soil is sadly neglected by gardeners who otherwise lovingly tend their plants. I have had many clients who were under the impression that soil tends itself, that it keeps on going year after year without need of care. Even in the country, where planting conditions are so much more favorable due to lack of pollution and ample sun, the soil needs periodic attention, because in a very few years it has a way of reverting back to its original properties. The average city soil is sorely deficient in valuable nutrients. Many gardens have only a few inches of good topsoil before you hit the hard subsoil. Only shallow-rooted annuals and ground covers can survive in shallow topsoil. At least one foot of topsoil is required for most plants, with larger shrubs and trees requiring well over two feet.

If you are the owner and you truly enjoy your garden and expect to get much use out of it for many years to come, you have to grit your teeth and get down to the business of improving the soil. It's good therapy for city tensions; there's nothing like sinking your hands into soil, even if it's poor soil. Knowing that you're in the process of turning it into good soil may make you feel you should have a halo over your head! Not only will your ego and your soul be rewarded, but so will your plants. Once you have finished, it's a matter of giving the soil "booster shots" every few years. Not that soil renovation must be a drastic job. For one thing, total renewal would be far too expensive in the city. Unlike the country, where you can buy topsoil and other ingredients by the carload and have them dumped on the property for you to use at your convenience, in the city you have to buy by the bag. No matter what it's called, "load" or what-have-you, it still has to be carted through the house in bags. But so little is needed by comparison that truckloads are not for city backyards. Your soil doesn't have to be totally removed and replaced; it needs to be cultivated, enriched and given proper drainage.

Let's start by analyzing the soil. This means testing its pH. City dwellers are becoming conscious of this term, if only because of its increased use in hair treatment. (Hair stylists for both men and women—not to mention shampoo products—are constantly telling us about the pH or acidity of our hair.) The pH of the soil tells how acid or alkaline it is. The scale for testing it runs from 0 to 14. Right in the middle, 7, is "neutral" soil, which can run from 6.5 to 7.5. Above 7.5 it's "alkaline" (on the sweet side); below 6.5 it's "acid." Most plants are not really all that fussy, but too far up or down the scale and you're in trouble.

City soil is on the acid side and getting progressively more so. An article in *The New York Times* in June 1974 reported that two ecologists had found a sharp increase of acidity in the rainfall over the eastern United States (and Europe as well). The "average acidity of rainwater has increased to about that of a tomato. In occasional extreme cases, rains have been found to be as acidic as pure lemon juice." The study was made by Dr. Gene E. Likens of Cornell University and Dr. F. Herbert Bormann of Yale University. Oddly enough, the increased acidity is the result of antipollution devices (smokestack particle removers and the use of very tall smokestacks), which "have transformed local soot problems into a regional acid rain problem." City gardeners have enough to cope with without lemon juice falling on their plants.

You can have your soil checked by a professional (if you hire a landscape designer, he'll do this automatically), or you can take soil samples and mail them to your local Agricultural Experiment Station or Agricultural Extension Service, but chances are you won't go to all that fuss. It's far easier to make the test yourself. Soil test kits are available at all garden supply stores. These kits come in all styles, sizes and prices. Since all you really want to test is the acidity of the soil (you don't need to know about all sorts of minerals and other soil ingredients that test kits can analyze), the simplest model is sufficient. The job involves nothing more than dipping a piece of treated paper in the soil or mixing soil with a special liquid in a tiny bottle. Depending on the color the paper turns or the color of the liquid in the bottle, you know whether your soil is acid, neutral or alkaline. A color guide, part of the kit, indicates which is which. Since there is enough material in these kits to do dozens of tests, it's a good idea to do it every year and check on the constancy of your soil. As ecologists have discovered, urban conditions for horticulture change so rapidly that a yearly test is a good precaution to take. Besides, it's fun to test the soil yourself. You feel like a scientist and can really claim to know your garden from the ground up!

Once you know what kind of soil you have, you're ready to work on it. When you grab a handful, it should be loose, porous, yet with a rich feel to it, unlike a sandy soil which slips right through your fingers or a heavy one that feels like mud and won't leave your hand. It also should have a good smell, the way earth smells when you lie on it in a country meadow gazing at the clouds. Sour soil, often synonymous with city soil, doesn't refer to pH but to the heaviness, sour odor and lack of drainage that results from the lack of organic matter.

In order to remember approximately the degree of acidity, or lack of it, that plants like, the novice gardener can use the following thought association: plants in woodlands, swamps and moist shady areas like an acid soil; plants found in open fields and the country in general like a neutral to slightly acid soil; plants growing in hot, dry locations like an alkaline soil. Some examples of each group are: acid—wild flowers, azaleas, hollies, rhododendrons, pines, hemlocks, yews; neutral—most annuals, perennials, deciduous trees and shrubs, roses; alkaline—desert plants (cacti and succulents), alyssum, geraniums, carnations, morning glory, clematis.

Fortunately for city dwellers, their gardens rely heavily on acid-loving, evergreen shrubs for plant material, so that if the pH should read as low as 5 or even 4.5, this is perfectly suitable for rhododendrons, laurels and azaleas. There are chemicals, however, that change the soil to your exact specifications: aluminum sulfate or sulfur increases the acidity, while ground limestone makes it more alkaline. The addition of bone meal (high in nitrogen and phosphoric acid) to the soil is also a gentle, slow and beneficial way of increasing the alkalinity when there is need to raise it only slightly. Limestone is safe to use, as it will not burn plant roots even if used too liberally, whereas hydrated lime, faster to take effect, can injure plants. Follow directions on the package carefully when applying the products, and use a chemical only if the pH test indicates the need for it.

You'll quickly get the "feel" of your soil when you get your trusty hoe out and start cultivating. Dig into the soil as deeply as you can. Do you get clumps of earth or loose dirt? The way to lighten soil is to add either sand or perlite, about three inches, spread all over the surface and work well into the soil. I prefer perlite to sand because it's so much lighter to cart around and work with. It comes in large bags that even the tiniest woman can lift. Use a spade if the soil is really hard, and then use a metal rake to smooth the surface and break up the clumps (the flat back of the rake is great to break up the larger pieces).

Since you are doing all this digging anyway, now is a good time to incorporate some organic matter into the soil to ensure that it remains friable. "Leaf mold" and "humus" are the same and the terms can be used interchangeably. Leaf mold is peat, made of decomposed leaves, twigs and trunks of trees and shrubs. It's very acid when young or "raw" and can burn roots. It's fine when it's older and nearly black in color. The older kind is the only one you would be likely to buy already packaged. Peat moss, especially Michigan peat, is less acid than leaf mold. There are many kinds of peat, but the one most commonly used is derived from sphagnum mosses and from sedges (grasses). Peat moss helps retain moisture in the soil. Whether you use peat moss or humus depends on how acid your soil already may be and how available these products are locally. You can't go wrong using either, or a combination of both.

With the addition of sand (or perlite) and peat moss (or humus) to your soil, it should be a joy to look at. Raked to a smooth surface, it's ready for your lucky plants to sink their roots into. At this point, it's important to note that you cannot plant both acid-loving and alkaline-loving plants side by side in a small garden, whether of the city or country variety. The backbone of an urban garden is broad-leaved evergreens (hollies, rhododendrons, azaleas, laurels, andromedas) which *require* an acid soil, with needled evergreens (pines, hemlocks) trailing not too far behind in their liking for acid soil. Limestone and bone meal therefore should be applied judiciously near these plants, and only if the pH dips below 4.5. It's a different story where annuals and perennials are to be planted by themselves. Here the pH can be raised to meet their needs. Where shrubs and flowers share the same planters, whether ground-level or raised, select plants that are not too demanding in their soil requirements.

I'm all for saving labor, whether one's own or hired, and so rather than adding fertilizers later on, the smart thing to do is to add them when all your tools are out and you are digging up the whole garden. Preferably, fertilizers should be slow-releasing types so that they can benefit the soil over a long period of time. Cow manure is such a type, and so is superphosphate. Real cow manure is not only impossible to get in the city (and now in the country as well), but it's unpleasant to use. Dehydrated cow manure, however, comes in neat bags, is odorless (well, nearly) and is readily available, as is superphosphate. Always sprinkle a handful or two of superphosphate at the bottom of a hole before planting a tree or a shrub; it does wonders for them.

All types of plants benefit from dehydrated cow manure and superphosphate. Add them, according to package directions, to the soil when you add the perlite and peat moss. You will have such a glorious soil that your plants will have the strength to successfully fight off the harmful effect of city grime, soot and pollution which kill or stunt the growth of so many of them. Good soil preparation is well worth the effort and after all, you will be the one who reaps the benefits as you admire vigorous, healthy plants and free-blooming flowers. Little, if any, chemical fertilizers need be added over the years if the soil is well-prepared originally.

Obviously the time to do all this soil conditioning is when you acquire the property, but only if the soil can be worked easily. Winter is out of the question except in mild climates. Early spring is too soggy for the job—the soil is wet and you'll just make one enormous mud pie, which will harden and be a nightmare of a job to break up later on. But from mid-spring to late fall is perfect. Planting is done when best for the plants, but the beds can be ready so that all that will need to be done is raking the surface to loosen it so you can dig the holes for the plants.

12. MULCHES

A mulch is a material spread over the surface of the soil for the purpose of decoration (tying the whole garden scheme together) as well as for utilitarian reasons (soil conditioning, weed control, prevention of soil heaving during early spring thaws, moisture retention, and so forth). There are so-called winter mulches and summer mulches. Smart gardeners combine the whole works: a year-round mulch, one that is both attractive and beneficial to plants. Once put down, this mulch needn't be touched again, except for periodic replacement of what has been washed away by rain or assimilated into the soil. Nature's way of mulching is the leaves and pine needles which form a thick carpet every fall, and ground covers which grow wild. These natural mulches retain moisture in the ground during the summer; and after the first hard frost, they keep the soil cold all through the prematurely warm spells in early spring which lead to heaving of the ground and injury to surface roots.

The backyard garden is on display all year-round, and for this reason, mulching material should be decorative. These are some attractive mulches:

Buckwheat hulls have a soft brown color. Though small and lightweight, they don't blow easily in the wind. They absorb practically no moisture from the soil, yet allow the rainwater to filter through.

Stones are favorites for contemporary or Japanese gardens. They come in all sizes from tiny white marble chips to smooth beach rocks three to four inches in diameter—however, as with all mulches, the larger the size of the material, the deeper the application, to prevent weeds and ensure thorough coverage of the soil. When extra-large stones are used, it's thriftier to apply a layer of small ones first, topping off with the larger ones. Obviously, stones add nothing to the condition of the soil or to its nutrient value.

Shredded redwood or pine bark comes in fine texture or in large nuggets. These mulches are extremely decorative and blend well with any type of garden. If nuggets are used, it's best to use a layer of fine-textured bark as a foundation under the nuggets, as in the case of larger stones. Being rot-resistant, redwood does not break down as readily as pine and therefore does not add any organic matter to the soil.

Oak leaves are excellent for use around acid-loving rhododendrons and azaleas. Oak leaves don't mat (which causes rot), and makes them far better than other leaves.

Pine needles are also great for acid-loving conifers and broad-leaved evergreens. If you use leaves or pine needles around other plants, sprinkle the mulch with limestone each year to counteract the excessive acidity these give to the soil. It's really safer and wiser to limit their use only to acid-loving shrubs and trees.

Peat moss is not only expensive to use as a mulch, but it's not all that satisfactory, for it packs solidly as it dries out after a heavy rain. The next rainfall is unable to filter through unless the peat moss is broken up and wetted down. It's best to work peat moss into the soil when you are cultivating it rather than using it as a mulch. Besides, as with leaves, peat moss adds to the acidity of the soil and needs limestone to offset this.

Cocoa-bean hulls have a delicious chocolate aroma when first put down, but they cake in dry weather and become slimy after rain. In damp areas they develop an unattractive mold.

Peanut hulls, sawdust, wood chips, tobacco stems and ground corncobs are plentiful in some parts of the country, but they are not attractive. The same is true of salt hay and black plastic.

The best time to apply a mulch is in the early spring when the soil is still moist (after a heavy rain is ideal), after you have fertilized the plants and before the weeds have made their appearance. If any have popped up, pull them out before spreading the mulch. Leave the mulch on all year, adding to it as it breaks down and becomes part of the soil. Keep the mulch always three or four inches thick to be most effective; this obviously depends a great deal on the type used. The finer the mulch, the less you need. The objective is to let none of the soil show through so that light won't reach the soil and make it possible for weeds to pop up. Weeds must see light to grow.

Contrary to popular opinion, the reason for a mulch during the winter months is not to keep the soil warm. Quite the opposite: it's to keep the soil cold after it has frozen so that come those false warm days of January, the plants are not fooled into thinking spring has arrived. A mulch also prevents the frozen soil from heaving, which exposes roots to dry out and perish. When planting time comes around simply push the mulch to one side, dig the hole, put in the plant, and then spread the mulch back evenly around the plants.

13. WINTER PROTECTION

The backyard garden needs far less winter protection than does the terrace, exposed as the latter is to severe damaging winds. The year-round mulch previously mentioned serves, of course, as a winter mulch as well. Newly planted perennials benefit from a covering of leaves or evergreen branches (save your Christmas tree and other greens for this). Newly planted deciduous trees should have their trunks wrapped with the specially made pliable paper that expands with the tree as it grows, or with strips of burlap. Start winding at the top of the trunk, tying it securely at the bottom. Remove it after a year, as the tree will do nicely on its own thereafter.

As for evergreens (yew, spruce, hemlock, juniper, pine), nothing is more unattractive than the sight of these superb plants all bundled up in burlap. This is also true of such shrubs as holly, rhododendron, laurel, andromeda and azalea which also get the "sausage" treatment, the purpose of which is to prevent loss of excessive moisture in drying winds. Fortunately, science has come to our rescue with antitranspirant sprays, such as Wilt-pruf, which seal the pores of the foliage, holding the moisture in. One application in late fall and another in early spring will see the evergreens through (follow directions on the container, as it's important to spray only when the temperature is above 40 degrees. I also use this spray on my ivy, which frequently gets its leaves winter-killed. Now the leaves stay green and healthy-looking all through winter, with no loss of time and no waiting for new leaves to grow in order to replace the dead ones the following spring.

Obviously, judgment is important when deciding which plants should be sprayed. If you've had an evergreen in one corner for fifteen years and it has thrived through every type of winter, don't rush out and start spraying it. If your garden is well-sheltered on all sides, you have little worry concerning high winds. But do exercise extra care if yours is an exposed garden in the path of nasty, damaging winter and early spring winds, especially when it comes to newly planted conifers and broad-leaved evergreens.

If roses are well-mulched all year-around, there is little danger of winter damage, but if you're in doubt, simply mound extra soil at the base—about six inches will do.

Snow is called the "poor man's mulch" and is excellent on the ground. Unfortunately, in city gardens it rarely lasts for any length of time. But while snow is good on the soil, it's definitely not so on branches, as the weight may break them. Gently, very gently, shake the snow off with a broom or a towel. In the case of ice forming on the branches, don't touch it. You can do far more harm than good by trying to knock it off. If a limb is bent alarmingly low by ice, prop it up until the ice has melted.

14. SPRING CLEANUP

There isn't really terribly much to do. As with a home that is well-maintained all year-around, there is no need for a dramatic, exhausting cleanup once a year. Remove any evergreen boughs you may have placed over perennials, as well as any burlap screens. If you used an antitranspirant, it will slowly disappear on its own at the right time. Remove the soil mounds around roses.

What is most important is an inspection tour. Check first for any winter damage to tree limbs and branches of shrubs. Prune off anything that is damaged; if a branch is torn, cut it off neatly (see chapter 25). Check next to see if the mulch is still at an even depth and whether or not it needs a bit of replenishing. Look for cracks in the masonry of walls, planters, flooring. Is there damage to the awning or other overhead protection? Snip off dead ends of vines and ground covers. Give the shrubs a "bath" to clean off soot that has accumulated during the winter months. (Don't bathe them in the winter, as the water freezes on the foliage.)

Your garden should now be ready for nature to take over and start growing, full speed ahead. Later on, you'll add annuals where you spot "holes" in your garden scheme, for color all summer long. If you have a lawn, however tiny, fertilize it in early spring and again in early fall. Additional early summer and late fall fertilizing are only for those whose lawns are real disaster areas and need powerful help—but it works and is easier than starting a new lawn from scratch. However, in these days of expensive and scarce fertilizers, it might be wiser to convert that lawn into an attractive ground cover.

As for fertilizers, if the soil has been well-prepared (see chapter 11), it can go for a few years without additional fertilizing, but if it's been more than three years since such a thorough soil conditioning was done, it's a good idea to give some booster shots to the shrubs and perennials. In close quarters, where plants of differing needs are growing side by side, it's tricky to apply the appropriate fertilizer. Read labels and follow directions carefully. Acid fertilizers and iron chelates are strictly for acid-loving plants, such as evergreens. For other plants, such as perennials, use standard fertilizers combining all the important ingredients, or cultivate superphosphate into the soil. Bone meal is also very good. There is no need to go around collecting a dozen varieties of fertilizers. One for acid-loving plants and another all-around formula such as 4-12-4, which is good for lawns and flower gardens (including perennials and roses), are sufficient for the city gardener (and others too, for that matter). Apply them according to directions—usually two to three pounds per hundred square feet (or roughly one cupful per plant). When cultivating the soil around each plant, go easy with flowers, so as not to disturb the roots. Avoid pouring fertilizer against the stems or trunks of plants. Water deeply afterward or pray for rain. The numbers on fertilizer bags refer to the ratio of the three major ingredients: nitrogen, phosphorus and potash. In the formula 4-12-4, therefore, there is 4 percent nitrogen, 12 percent phosphorus and 4 percent potash. The rest, should you wonder, is made up of fillers—sand or a similar material—to make it easier to spread.

Gardening in the Sky: Balconies, Terraces, Penthouses, Rooftops

When planting boxes at the edge of balconies, let the vines fall on the outside, as well as the inside, to give pleasure to those walking down below and
living across the street. Vines soften balconies and add greatly to the appearance of the building as a whole.
George Taloumis

15. PLANNING YOUR EXTERIOR DECORATING

Just as a terrace in the country can be any size and shape, so it can be in the city, although it's located high in the sky. This is true of the city terrace, but with the tremendous popularity of condominiums across the nation, a terrace can be both high above the ground and in a suburban environment as well! Real estate agents prefer the "terrace" to "balcony," as the former connotes larger space, but most apartment terraces are really balconies. The smaller ones are sometimes little more than "bureau drawers sticking out of the building," but even these are precious to tenants who gladly pay the extra rent for the privilege of stepping outdoors, lounging in the sun, eating alfresco and enjoying the view.

The moment one can walk around it with ease and set out several pieces of furniture, including a table, one can call this area a terrace. It can be very spacious, wrapping itself around the corner to another side of the building, providing several entrances to rooms facing onto it.

The difference between a terrace and a penthouse is purely one of locality. If the terrace is on the top floor of a building, it's a penthouse, no matter what its size. The connotation of penthouse, thanks to Hollywood, is that it must always be enormous, way up in the sky, on kissing terms with stars come nightfall when the full glamour treatment comes on. These fabulous penthouses do exist in large cities, but tiny terraces perched on top of low buildings also qualify as penthouses. Because there is no overhead shelter of any kind, penthouses have a severe wind problem. Not that terraces don't, but generally these have another terrace (or balcony) directly above them, or at least the side of the building, as some kind of protection against the wind. The penthouse, however, is open to the sky and highly vulnerable to the elements.

A rooftop terrace is really a penthouse, except that it's not on a tall building. It's found on a garage or a private house. It's literally "on top of the roof" and was not designed with gardening in mind. Sunbathing is about all the use most rooftop terraces are ever put to. But occasionally a frustrated gardener will set about bravely and successfully to transform this unused space into a little oasis of green plants and a few comfortable chairs. Only the building structure and the weight the rooftop can hold need restrict the ambitious gardener.

Whatever category your particular garden in the sky falls into, you will need some sort of plan before going out and buying plants and furnishings. It's exactly the same thing you would do with interior decorating; you'd take measurements before buying a wall unit or a large couch. That additional space outdoors is costing the apartment dweller—whether he be tenant or owner—plenty of extra money, so every inch of space has to be put to good use.

No two people have the same idea about what constitutes "good use" of a terrace (or a balcony, penthouse or rooftop, but for the sake of brevity, I'll use the word "terrace" to cover all of these). Some people enjoy gardening for its own sake, and to them a terrace offers the opportunity to grow plants they can't successfully grow indoors. Others are sun freaks and all they really want from their terrace is a gorgeous tan. Or they're "watchers" who enjoy looking down at the hustle and bustle of the city, the constant movement and changes of street scenes. (If they also sport a good pair of field glasses they're "voyeurs" as well!) For the majority, a terrace is an extra room, an outdoor living room to be enjoyed during the summer months, or all year-around for those lucky people living in mild climates. They want to read, snooze, eat, entertain, watch TV and daydream on this little bit of outdoors.

Knowing what you want most from your terrace is the first step to good planning. Analyze your needs and those of others living in the apartment and decide on the functions of the terrace. Is it to be

1. A place to read? You'll need a comfortable chair.
2. A place to eat alfresco? You'll need a table and as many chairs as there are members of the family. If space permits, make it a round table with an umbrella and add a barbecue.
3. A place to lounge and/or sunbathe? You'll need chaise longues.
4. A place to pursue your gardening hobby? Go easy on furniture to leave more room for two- and three-tier planters, containers, a workbench and a window greenhouse if there is space.
5. A place to entertain friends? (You'll need a serving table to hold buffet dishes and cocktail snacks and as many chairs and small tables as space permits.
6. A spot to enjoy a quiet predinner cocktail and a breath of fresh air? A couple of chairs and a small table will suffice.
7. A play area for small children? Leave as much free space as possible for a tricycle, sandbox, toys, etc. There should be adult supervision at all times, so have at least one comfortable chair.
8. An outdoor garden to be admired from inside the apartment only? Skip the furniture and just have plants, plants and more plants.

It's pretty obvious, from the suggested uses to which a terrace can be put, that the basic furnishings for two people revolve around two comfortable armchairs with two small side tables to hold books, drinks and ashtrays, or one larger table to be shared. Anything beyond this basic arrangement depends on the size of the terrace and the life-style of the occupants.

If yours is a very small balcony, there will be room only for window boxes (tied securely on top of the balcony railing but inside the perimeter of the balcony) to be filled with colorful annuals and trailing vines. Add a container with a shrub at one end and three or four pots of flowers grouped at the other end. Avoid a "matched" look at both ends of the balcony.

"Sunning" rather than gardening inspired the design of this rooftop garden in San Francisco's crowded Telegraph Hill. Containers of flowers soften the bold contemporary angles. Note the clever use of roll-up awning.
California Redwood Association

A narrow floor planter along the width of the terrace takes up less room than several large round containers, yet it provides more space for planting. If there is a bare wall to cover, use a narrow but deep floor planter to hold a vine. The planter can be as deep as needed, since there's no problem about utilizing space vertically. Insert a lattice frame into the planter to train the vine. If the balcony is so narrow that it's strictly standing-room-only with no space for furniture, concentrate on window boxes all around the edge of the balcony, with lots of hanging vines mixed in with the flowers. These vines form a soft green "wall" when seen from inside the apartment, a far prettier sight than staring at a solid brick wall or whatever is used for the balcony railing.

It's a must to check with your landlord about what you are allowed to construct and the weight that your terrace will hold. Don't be guided by what the former tenants or the next-door neighbors had on their terrace. They may not have taken this necessary precaution, but *you* should, for your own safety and peace of mind, not to mention lawsuits in case of falling plants. Masonry beds filled with soil are tremendously heavy, especially when watered. However, as you'll see, there are ways to get around the weight problem.

If space permits, a tree should have top priority in your planning scheme, not only because it's beautiful, but because a tree also provides shade and interest to the design. Plants which are all the same height are monotonous, no matter how handsome they are. A tree on a city or country terrace becomes the dominant factor to which all other plants are scaled for size and form, to design a garden that is in harmony with its surroundings. A tree is the visual connecting link between the building and the outdoors. Large terraces can accommodate several trees, each one a focal point for a different "living area."

As with plants, avoid flower beds or containers that are all the same height and shape. Again, space decides how much variety you may have, but if you own your apartment, it's worth the expense to build in at least one masonry planter (one or two tiers). Planters with gently curving edges are more pleasing to the eye. The easiest and dreariest-looking design is one where all the planters follow the lines of the terrace, hugging the walls, adding no architectural beauty. If you rent the apartment, simulate the look

The tiniest terrace or balcony can be turned into an oasis with a grouping of potted plants. Or, get similar results with window boxes tightly secured and resting on the *inside* of the balcony. Fill the boxes with colorful annuals and vines.

George Taloumis

of built-ins with groupings of round and square containers, breaking up the line of the usual rectangular boxes.

Restraint is the key word when introducing variety in planters. Avoid harsh, sudden changes of designs. A terrace has to be enormous to handle several kinds of building materials in planters. If this is the case, treat the terrace as you would a country garden, creating several gardens-within-a-garden: a little nook here for quiet conversation, a shady spot there for reading and lounging, a spacious area for dining and entertaining. Free-form or symmetrical "island" planters help to define traffic patterns, as does a change in the design of the flooring to indicate a path. A large terrace can look like a cold, barren piazza if it is planted only along its edges with the center left bare.

A pool or a fountain, however small, adds tremendous charm to a terrace, as does a handsome piece of statuary strategically placed to create a point of interest or to draw the eye toward a spectacular view. Only your budget limits what can be done with your terrace, which brings us to a word about cost. Gardening in the city is expensive because everything has to be trucked in from the country and then delivered to your home (while the delivery van is double parked and gets a ticket). Service elevators are not always available for the length of time you need them, and the men may have to make many trips to your floor to deliver soil, containers, plants and other materials. All this takes time . . . and time costs money.

Yet, when one considers the cost of doing an average-sized terrace versus the similar cost of decorating a living room, the expense is no longer shocking. If an apartment dweller is to derive the greatest pleasure from his terrace, he should think of it as one more room to decorate. I have seen apartments that have been decorated in exquisite taste, with no thought on the part of the owners of saving money or cutting corners. But their terraces are skimpily planted, forlorn-looking if not downright dowdy, totally out of keeping with the mood and style of the interiors. The potential of the terrace is totally ignored.

If the owner of an apartment doesn't care for the outdoors, he should consider converting the terrace into an enclosed solarium, a greenhouse-without-plants with wicker furniture and colorful fabrics, a place to be enjoyed year-round. But if the occupants

Statuary need not be earthbound. Use them with vines on a wall for maximum effect.
George Taloumis

If you live in the north and a year-round garden is what you want, turn your terrace into a greenhouse. It is easily installed, but be sure to get the landlord's consent first.
Lord & Burnham

of the apartment *do* enjoy the terrace as an outdoor extension of their home, they should be willing to pay the cost, which can be spread over several years, as with any landscaping or interior decorating expense. Most of the investment is in one-time-only construction of built-in planters, an awning, permanent planting material such as trees and shrubs and outdoor furniture. Even the soil, when properly mixed, lasts for many years, needing only occasional "boosts." Containers and window boxes also last for years, if solidly built and reasonably cared for. The chief yearly expense thereafter is for annuals and fertilizer. In defense of cliff dwellers, it should be said that in the country one also sees magnificent homes which are examples of fine architecture, with tastefully designed interiors, but surrounded by sadly neglected gardens.

When you are planning the terrace, thought must be given to its maintenance. For reluctant, lazy and/or rich gardeners, there are services that take over the upkeep of your terrace, but for most people, part of the delight of having a terrace is to care for the plants, check their progress, watch them grow, all the time marveling at the wonders of Mother Nature and at the gallant struggle plants wage to survive their hostile urban environment. To have a plant "make it" and flourish year after year gives one a tremendous feeling of satisfaction, even for the most undedicated gardener.

For gardeners who rent their apartments and understandably don't wish to go to the expense of built-in planters, containers are a good substitute. These come in many styles, sizes and shapes (see chapter 19). Grouping several large pots or containers in one area is more attractive than having them scattered about the terrace. Round containers soften the angularity of the long flower boxes that are the backbone of terrace gardening. If sufficiently sheltered, hanging baskets are always a delightful addition to any garden, and they take no floor space!

Once you have decided what kind of terrace you want, what its chief purpose is to be, you will be able to be more specific about your needs, making your shopping list that much easier to compile (not to mention saving money because you'll know *what* you want and *where* it's to go on the terrace, so there'll be less chance of costly mistakes). If you have no place to store outdoor furniture (and who does?), buy the sturdy, weather-resistant kind that will last for many years without upkeep worries. Spot-resistant, sunproof fabrics that won't fade after one summer are also high on the list of items to be considered. Cast-iron furniture is far too heavy for city terraces, and wicker and canvas are hard to keep clean. The world of plastics has seen such giant strides in the last decade that the selection of furniture is bewildering and most is made of low-maintenance materials.

You usually get what you pay for when it comes to quality, but do inquire about maintenance requirements (easy-to-care-for furniture and high prices don't always go together; you can pay a lot for a chair that will be a nightmare to keep clean). Aluminum furniture with vinyl webbing is the most popular today—though by no means the least expensive—but it's a good buy. Very light furniture is not practical for a windy terrace unless you want it to land in your living room or on your neighbor's terrace (more law-suits). Even a sturdy umbrella table should have its umbrella folded when not in use, or it could make like Mary Poppins in stormy weather.

When planning the terrace, you can indulge your personal taste when it comes to selecting furniture, but unfortunately you can't do the same when buying plants. What will grow in the *city* and on *your terrace* has to be considered first and foremost. This limits your selection of plants, but there are still plenty available. (See plant charts for details.)

Since evergreen shrubs form the mainstay of terrace planting, these should be chosen most carefully, not only for their suitability to terrace culture but also for variety in their leaf texture. Six shrubs all alike are a monotonous sight. Six shrubs all different would be even worse, as this would resemble the showroom of a city nursery. Hedges and borders are in a different category. They must obviously all match, not only in variety, but in size as well.

Try to have shrubs in more than one shade of green; nature provides so many different ones. Let your eye be the judge. The best way of choosing shrubs that will be planted together in a fairly close area is to group them at the nursery, stand back and take a good long look. Is one dwarfed by the others? Is the dainty foliage of one shrub totally obscured by the boldness of another? Would one be shown off better as a specimen by itself in a con-tainer? Reason the same way you would in a department store when shopping for indoor furniture. Plants also have personalities, and some just don't go together. Generally, plants that grow wild in the same locality look good next to one another—pines with ferns and mosses, or fruit trees with field flowers. Line, form, mood, all combine to create a design that can be either pleasing or jarring to the eye. Some evergreens have a formal look, a certain compact growth habit that goes well with clipped hedges, box-wood or symmetrical flower beds.

If your terrace is large enough to take in a tree, you are indeed fortunate, for this adds much to a garden. A deciduous tree contributes dramatically to the landscape, providing shade for the terrace, flowers in the spring and berries in the fall (if you choose one of the right varieties), a dominant focal point setting the scale for the garden and "connecting" it with the building, cool-looking airy greenery as your eyes look upward toward the skyline (which is a pretty regular occupation on a terrace). Such a tree needs space, however, not only vertically but horizontally. It spreads on all sides if it's good and healthy, even when it's a tub-grown, top-pruned dwarf variety. For this reason, take careful measurements before ordering your tree, making sure that you have enough room to make it happy. If not, there are many good-looking shrubs that look almost like small trees but require less space. Most trees involuntarily turn into dwarf varieties when their roots become restricted. Unlike their country cousins, which can reach deep into the earth for nutrients and water with no limit to their root growth, terrace trees have a handicap when it comes to planting depth. They can make it nonetheless, but in somewhat reduced size.

A tree is a major purchase and will give you many years of pleasure. It's also costly, which makes me urge you to have it planted by the nursery from which you bought it. You will probably buy only one tree, perhaps two, but these are permanent, once-only investments (as compared with other plants). The container for it must be wider than the rootball of the tree, to prevent it from becoming root-bound too soon. Planting a mature tree (around six feet) is heavy work and difficult to do on a terrace. Since you are spending so much for the tree to begin with, add a bit more and let the nursery be responsible for proper planting, which ensures its future health. It's a different story when it comes to very young trees (whips) or shrubs. These you can handle yourself or with the help of a friend.

When choosing a tree, if privacy is a problem and for some reason fencing doesn't solve it, an evergreen may be a better choice than a deciduous tree. Evergreens are denser and their entirely different growth habit makes them perfect for screening purposes. Teamed with broad-leaved evergreen shrubs, they form a "voyeur-proof" wall. You may prefer an evergreen tree anyway if you are especially winter-minded: loving the look of snow on the branches (but not for too long, as it can break them), or feeling depressed by the sight of a leaf-bare terrace. If yours is a very large terrace, combining both deciduous and evergreen trees is ideal landscaping. You can have the best of both worlds in limited space, however, with a dwarf flowering fruit tree (such as a crab apple or a Japanese cherry) teamed with evergreen shrubs. Scale is important, as one plant (the tree) should stand out clearly as the dominant factor, with surrounding shrubs as supporting players. If tall shrubs vie for attention with a smallish tree, none comes out the winner, and the design of the garden is dull and undistinguished.

Shrubs are the backbone of any garden—city or country—and so should not be chosen at random. Group together two or three of the same kind but of different varieties and sizes to create excitement—for example, three hollies of varying height, width and leaf patterns. Andromedas also come in different varieties; three or more of these can be grouped attractively to make a beautiful year-round green garden.

It makes sense to have several identical shrubs together when you want to dramatize another spectacular shrub—making it the star of your garden. By keeping everything around the specimen shrub low-key, you let it bask in the spotlight. An example of this could be a handsome Scotch pine surrounded by dwarf andromedas.

If a poll were taken among terrace owners asking their chief reason for having a terrace, the predominant reply would most likely be to get the feeling of escape from the city. The gardener feels that ultimate success in designing a terrace has been achieved when he can stretch out on a chaise, pick up a book and, before starting to read, look around him and see nothing that reminds him of the city. He might as well be in a corner of a country garden. Sounds incredible? Not at all. There are many city terraces with such lush foliage in mid-summer that only when one is standing is one brought back to reality. The clever use of vines climbing on walls, hedges facing parapets, trees and shrubs, flowers, attractive patio paving, awnings hiding surrounding buildings, contribute to the illusion of being miles away.

Check the following points when planning your terrace:

1. Is there room for a tree? If so, what kind, and where would

be the best place for it? No two terraces have exactly the same view, so it's difficult to generalize. If the terrace wraps around the building, the corner is a good spot. Will it be in a tub or planted directly in a built-in bed?

2. How many shrubs are needed to frame the terrace with greenery? Will these take the form of a hedge, or will the shrubs be in informal groupings? If they are grown in beds, will there be room at their base for flowers? There should be space for shallow-rooted annuals if the bed is wide enough; if not, shrubs and flowers should be planted separately.

3. Where is color needed to brighten the terrace? That's where flowers should be planted. On window boxes attached to the parapet? At the base of shrubs? In their own tubs or planters? In individual pots grouped together in one area? Decide how you will plant your annuals, and then figure out how many you'll need and what color scheme you want to use. If you want to grow perennials, make sure the planters and/or containers are at least twelve inches deep and that you have filled them with good rich soil. Perennials are going to stay in that soil for a long time and need the nutrients that only top-quality ingredients contribute. They'll have to be combined with annuals if you want color all summer long, because perennials bloom for relatively short periods. Only if your terrace is very large will you have enough space to plant the many different kinds of perennials you would need to have successive blooming all summer long.

4. Is there space for a vine somewhere? Vines are so graceful that it would be a pity not to have at least one. On the fence? Up the building wall? They can also hang *down* from window boxes or tubs filled with annuals. Don't plant them at the base of trees or shrubs, as they will compete for room and nutrients.

5. Do you have use for a ground cover? If your terrace is too large (poor you!) and you have little time to maintain it, plant "green" beds of ground covers with spring bulbs in their midst and your worries are over. Trees and shrubs will take care of vertical interest.

Not everyone has room for all of the plant categories I've listed, but checking off which ones apply to you is a good way of seeing how much you can fit in. Sometimes the obvious is easily overlooked. The building wall is frequently left totally unused, yet it could have a vine growing against it, or containers with hanging plants could be fastened to the wall with special metal holders. A window opening onto the terrace can have its own flower box.

All of these are "off the floor" plantings which take up none of the precious space needed for outdoor furniture. Even furniture can be put to use as planters, whether it's built for just that purpose (one-, two- and three-tiered wrought-iron styles) or a regular glass-topped table holding a number of pots. Again, group the pots whenever possible. Scattering one here and one there is a total loss. No "statement" is made from a decor point of view. Leave an unusually handsome specimen plant by itself, but others are best kept together.

Where built-in masonry beds are not feasible, a three-tiered effect can be achieved by having one row of large identical tubs filled with matching columnar evergreens (tall and narrow) forming a hedge, then alternating a second row of smaller tubs with a variety of shrubs in front of the first row, finishing with a third front row of squat pots filled with flowers. The three rows of descending heights form a cascade arrangement that can be changed and moved around at will and can be taken by the tenant when he moves out of the apartment.

Last, but nevertheless important, on the list of things to remember when designing a terrace is storage space for tools, soil, fertilizers, etc. If the terrace is large enough, a small shed can be built in an out-of-the-way corner, behind some shrubbery. It can be little more than a large wooden box with a lid. For smaller areas, try a version of the deacon's bench, with a seat that folds up to reveal a good deal of storage space underneath. I have such a bench in the potting shed of my greenhouse and it houses a lot of small items. It can easily store all the fertilizers and small tools necessary.

Unless you buy in very large quantities, you're not likely to have huge bags of soil to store. You will have used up the soil and other ingredients when you did all your planting. Whatever may be left over can be stored in heavy plastic bags (the kind used for outdoor garbage cans) and kept hidden inside wicker hampers. If the wicker is painted a dark color, such as forest green, it will not show the soot and dirt. It's hard to keep wicker spotless, but it takes kindly to rain, which keeps it from becoming brittle and breaking. I hose down my indoor wicker furniture periodically for just this reason.

A large plastic sheet or tarpaulin is a must to spread on the terrace when potting plants and mixing soil. It's also good to have on hand when you have deliveries of plants which must be brought through the living room en route to the terrace. Place the plants on the clean plastic and drag the whole thing through the room. Country gardeners can afford to be messy—in fact, that's part of the fun for them—but city gardeners have no choice but to be neat and tidy, unless they don't mind large rug-cleaning bills and tiring moppings-up of the terrace.

Drainage is rarely a problem with terraces, because they are constructed with specific gardening use in mind. Water has to drain somewhere when you turn on the hose; therefore, terraces are equipped with drain outlets as well as outside water faucets to which you connect your hose. Keep it connected all the time (except in winter) so that watering is a quick and easy chore, since daily watering and syringing of plants is a must during very hot weather.

16. FENCES—WALLS

Many terraces are balconies which extend individually from the building line, with no other terrace adjoining them. These terraces frequently have railings made of a transparent material which allows maximum light. Additional side-fencing on such terraces would be for wind and/or absolute privacy.

In the case of wind, the higher your location, the stronger it is. If you can't sit comfortably on your terrace on a mildly windy day (mild, that is, down at street level), you may be sure that your plants aren't going to like it either. For your sake as well as theirs, secure a fence of woven saplings or some other material to the side from which the wind blows. A vine will cover the fence in no time. Whatever type of fence is installed, however, it should not be totally airtight. There should be enough openwork to prevent the full force of the wind from knocking it down.

The desire for privacy beats far stronger in the breast of the city dweller than in his country cousin's. Perhaps it's because privacy in general has always been one of the city's great advantages over small-town living. Even if the nearest terrace to yours is two or three apartments away, if the tenants are overly interested in your barbecue menu or keeping track of how many drinks you're having, you may want fencing installed to keep your peace of mind (and to keep them guessing). If wind is no factor, a screen of simple trellis work is effective and attractive with a vine growing against it.

Larger terraces have even greater need of wind protection for plants, and they too may have a privacy problem. As for penthouses, located as they are on the top floor, there is no problem with next-door neighbors (except where there is an adjoining penthouse), but there is certainly a problem with wind. An ordinary windy day on the street becomes a raging storm on the thirtieth floor.

Any kind of openwork fence will do as long as it is sturdy and properly installed. As with masonry work, any fencing job (other than for tiny balconies) should be done by a professional. Secure anchorage is vital to withstand sudden tornado-like gusts of wind, and unless you're skilled at this kind of work, you'd better let an expert do it. On a side of the terrace which is not too windy, plant a hedge of shrubs.

Stockade fencing is the most popular type. It's made of woven saplings, and its rustic look blends well with plants. But there are also other kinds of fences available to suit individual tastes and budgets. The supplier will be only too delighted to show you samples of his product and give you an estimate.

The only type of masonry wall a terrace dweller might need is one to separate the service area or play area from the rest of the terrace. These walls are fairly low and ornamental, usually of brick. Weight, as with any construction done on a terrace, has to be carefully considered. On a large terrace, where different areas created for specific leisure purposes adjoin one another, a well-

Add a vine to the flowers in your floor boxes and the fencing will be quickly covered.
Muriel Orans

placed screen of shrubs is sometimes more attractive and functions equally as a wall. A permanent wall may be considered between two large terraces or penthouses, but usually the building has taken care of this matter long ago. Get permission from the management for any masonry work (for structural and legal reasons), and remember that such work should be undertaken only by a professional.

17. FLOORS

Fortunately, flooring is already installed when you take possession of your terrace. The floor is designed with the specific functions of a terrace in mind, so you don't have to worry about such things as drainage, water seeping into the apartment, etc. Older terraces need periodic repairs and the management takes care of it, or, if you are the owner, you have to have a professional do the job.

In the case of the very small terrace, indoor-outdoor carpeting can cover tiny cracks and stains on the cement floor. This type of carpeting has come a long way since it first came out, and it is now available in many colors and designs. However, water drainage is not very efficient and the illusion of "outdoors" is lost. If possible, it's best to keep flooring as naturalistic as possible and not have it compete with the plants which are, together with the view of the city, the main assets of any high-rise terrace. A handsome suggestion: the rugged beauty of a redwood deck can be duplicated in miniature on a terrace by installing just a small section of it over the existing flooring.

When money is no object and you yearn for a super, glamorous terrace that has an Old World aura to it, you can install a magnificent floor design of imported tiles. These tiles range from solid colors to intricate designs, used alone or combined. But be prepared to pay handsomely for this luxury—you had better own the apartment, rather than rent it.

Old rooftops, never meant to be terraces in the first place, present a very real flooring problem. Expert help is needed to transform one into a safe and functional garden. If it will take the weight, and this *must* be checked with the building owners, it will require a covering of concrete or asphalt, which is then topped with bricks, roofing slates, pea gravel or fir bark. The last two are the lightest in weight. Or a redwood deck can be built, if a contemporary look is desired. Proper drainage is essential to make the rooftop absolutely waterproof, as well as to avoid puddles after each rainfall.

18. OVERHEAD SHELTER

The usefulness of a terrace, no matter what its size, is enormously increased when it offers shelter from the elements. Rain sends everybody indoors, and too much sun or wind does the same thing. To these add soot, ever-present in large cities. Installation of some kind of overhead protection gives the owners of a terrace insurance against last-minute disappointments when entertaining.

The design of many modern buildings is such that a terrace is usually sheltered by the terrace on the floor above. Larger terraces, however, are usually on the setbacks of buildings, leaving them exposed to the skies, as are penthouses and rooftops. Some sort of overhead shelter is needed in these cases. An awning is the logical choice because it can be rolled up or down as the occasion demands; it's certainly kept rolled up in the winter so as not to be torn to shreds by the high winds or to buckle under heavy snows. Dining alfresco, which is one of the many charms that a terrace offers, does not become a game of Russian roulette with the dark clouds; nor does one have to gulp the food quickly before it becomes covered with soot.

An awning should be installed by an expert, who will also advise you about the proper type to get. Wind velocity, exposure and location of the terrace are all important factors when selecting the appropriate awning, and only professionals in the field can give you the correct information based on your particular needs.

If you never eat outdoors and hate shade like poison, an awning is probably an unnecessary luxury, but it becomes a requirement for those who spend a great deal of time on their terrace and want to be able to choose between sun and shade.

A trellis or an arbor is a decorative choice for partial cover when all you want is to cut down the sun's rays. But forget the dainty treillage-type design; the wind will make mincemeat of this in no time flat. Only sturdy metal can withstand the wind's velocity on high floors. Let a vine cover the arbor for additional screening plus beauty, as well as to create a shady nook for outdoor furniture. A redwood lath-type shelter is excellent for a low roof-top where wind is not a problem. These are all sturdy, permanent installations and best suited for those who are owners of the apartment or who have a long lease.

A word of caution about awnings and plants: when the rain beats down on an awning, it pours down its sides and drowns any plant in its way. Make sure, when the awning is put up, that there are no built-in beds directly under the sides. Containers only have to be moved a few inches away to avoid this problem. You may think that it would be one way of watering plants, but the cascading water makes deep ridges in containers and forms gullies in the soil of beds.

A bonus of a permanent awning or a partial cover is that it's a perfect vehicle for hanging baskets, making it possible to have still more plants without taking up precious floor space. Also, since one is usually seated or eating under an awning, one can admire these hanging baskets at close range. The baskets form a very pretty enclosure to the awning when they hang on either side. Plant a few long, trailing vines in the baskets for a touch of lushness and a cool feeling on a hot day.

19. PLANTERS AND CONTAINERS

The first consideration a terrace-owner faces, come planting time, is what to put plants in. Should it be a built-in masonry bed, or a container (ready-made or made-to-order)? The majority are able to solve this problem quickly because most terraces are not large enough to warrant permanent masonry, which takes up far more room than do containers. The beauty of curved and straight masonry planters is that they are an architectural part of the terrace, of imposing dimensions and ideally suited for larger plants. There is no point in having a tiny masonry bed made-to-order. The cost simply isn't in proportion to the results one gets. Which brings us to cost: there is no doubt that anything made-to-order is expensive. A skilled mason has to do the job if it's to last for a long time.

I strongly advise anyone going in for this type of construction work to retain the services of a landscape designer. After the beds are built, there can be no second guessing about their proper location, as one can do with containers. It's too late to do anything about it if it all looks wrong and out of proportion to the overall size of the terrace. Beds of graceful curves should be teamed with rectangular ones to avoid monotony, and tiered beds are used for vertical interest (and extra planting space), all for the purpose of balance and unity in the design of the terrace. Get construction estimates from the landscape designer before you go ahead. Consider a combination of one or two built-in beds with containers to cut down on the expense.

Brick is the most popular and versatile material used, although concrete blocks are also available and suitable. When painted white, bricks take on an entirely different look, sometimes even more attractive than the usual red color. Bricks and plants have a natural affinity for one another. Special attention must be given to proper drainage ("weep holes" as they are called) in the walls of higher beds. If not sturdily built with the right "pitch," retaining walls may crack during the winter under pressure from the soil. (That's why you need a mason who knows his business.) It's important to have cracks and other faults repaired as quickly as possible, before they become major and therefore expensive jobs.

Trees and shrubs grow with the years, so it's wise to have the planters built as wide and as deep as possible. A depth of about three feet is needed for trees and large shrubs, two feet for perennials and small shrubs and one foot for annuals. These depths will prevent plants from drying out too fast and will save you much watering time.

Weight is an important factor when one is considering masonry beds. They are a great deal heavier than wood containers, so it's imperative to check with the building owner to see if the terrace floor will take it. Since cost is another factor, much depends on whether you own or rent your apartment. Most city

Tiered planters break the monotony of floor planters along walls and provide maximum space for flowers as well. If properly constructed, they should last for many, many years.
Gottscho-Schleisner, Inc.

dwellers rent theirs, although with condominiums sweeping the country, this picture is rapidly changing.

Look into the possibility of using Featherock, fiber glass rocks or some other lightweight material in place of masonry if weight is the only reason holding you back from built-ins. There are so many new products coming out each year in the "look-alike" field that "imitation" rocks cemented together not only cut down dramatically on weight, but are almost impossible to distinguish from natural stones.

Wood containers come in all sizes and shapes. Many are ready-made; others have to be made to your specifications. You can take them with you when you move and you can change them around as you would furniture when you tire of a particular layout. Floor planters hold flowers, vines, vegetables and small shrubs, while large tubs and barrels are for trees and the bigger shrubs. To create the illusion of a garden, group containers of various sizes and heights. Just as a masonry bed looks handsomest in the corner of a terrace, so would a group of three tubs, the largest holding a small tree, the others planted with medium and smaller shrubs. On either side, add long rectangular boxes filled with flowers to complete the corner. Scale is important in grouping containers, in order not to have smaller ones overwhelmed by the larger tubs. A beautiful tree is best by itself in a corner, flanked by a hedge or by window boxes of flowers on the parapet. Smaller containers and plants need each other's company to look important and to create the greenery of a garden. If they are spottily scattered around the terrace, no focal point is created.

There is an endless variety of containers. Redwood, cypress and red cedar are the longest-lasting and most rot-resistant of the wood containers. Woods such as pine and oak need a coat of wood preservative. Old whiskey barrels are sensational for trees and come in several sizes suitable for shrubs as well. For the contemporary look, there are synceram planters with a fiber glass coating, extremely lightweight, with smooth or textured finish. Also available are plastic (transparent or opaque), porcelain, enamel, terra-cotta and soy tubs (wood bound with bamboo strips). But no matter which kind you choose, *all* must have drainage holes at the bottom.

Glazed pottery is better than unglazed because it retains

moisture longer, requiring less watering. Another trick is to keep the plant in a large ordinary plastic pot and then to place the pot inside an ornamental clay pot or Italian-style terra-cotta urn. However, as already mentioned, there are some very attractive contemporary plastic containers to choose from, which are worth the extra expense for one special plant or two. When one gets to large-sized pots (anything fourteen inches or more in diameter), prices are going to be high, so caution and planning beforehand are advisable when it comes to the style of planter you desire and the size of the plants.

If your terrace will support the weight, nothing is more formal in an "Italian Riviera" mood than ornate concrete planters and urns, especially when teamed with statuary and a fountain. Not as glamorous but in the same vein are terra-cotta or clay pots; some come in highly decorative styles, but it should be noted that they may crack during winter thaws when the soil heaves. Reinforced fiber glass planters and containers look like concrete but, as already stated, are far lighter. These are best for a contemporary look. For those who are undecided, nothing takes the place of wood. It goes with everything and is lightweight. Wood planters and tubs, together with several large clay pots, take care of the plantings of most terraces.

To allow for proper drainage and good air circulation, and to prevent rotting (in the case of wood), planters should be raised one inch or so from the floor. Pots can sit on gravel in their matching saucers, which looks very attractive as well. As for larger planters, wooden slats (one-by-two-inch) can be placed underneath to raise them inconspicuously from the floor. Using bricks under containers is the easiest way out but doesn't look very attractive. In a pinch, however, bricks can be screened with small potted plants grouped at the base of the tub. Some containers come with their own "dollies," which solves the problem neatly. If you place wood tubs on gravel, make sure the gravel is two to three inches thick, minimum, so that when it rains the wood won't sit in water and rot.

Don't compromise on size when it comes to buying planters and containers. Plants suffer when their roots are constricted. If weight or your budget prevents you from buying a large container, select a smaller plant or buy a less expensive but large enough container. Pine is the least expensive of the woods, and, while not as long-lasting as the others, it will do the job very nicely, especially for those who rent their apartments. Stay away from cheap metal boxes. They have no insulation against heat or cold and they're much too small for plants to grow well.

When arriving at a budget for the terrace, take the cost of containers into consideration; it's foolish to spend a great deal of money on fine quality plants, especially permanent ones like trees and shrubs, and not to house them in adequate and attractive boxes. Think of the plant and its container as one unit, with the cost of the box in proportion to the cost of the plant. A fine specimen plant which is the proud focal point of your terrace needs matching quality in its container to be properly shown off.

20. PUTTING THE PLAN ON PAPER

You've analyzed your needs and what you expect from your terrace. You've decided how much you want to spend to furnish the terrace with plants, containers and furniture. The budget can be extended over several years. As with furnishing a home, not everything is purchased at the same time unless one wants instant gratification and has unlimited funds!

You're now familiar with the need for and types of fences available, as well as flooring, overhead protection and the containers necessary to hold the plants. What comes next is putting it all together . . . on paper. This prevents costly mistakes later on. It's wise to make your errors on paper first. You might think that a plan is only needed for a backyard garden or an enormous penthouse, but *any* terrace beyond the size of a balcony needs a few "roughs" drawn before you go out and buy furnishings.

A sheet of graph paper and a few sheets of tracing paper will be all you'll need, plus a pencil and an eraser. Let each square on the graph paper equal one square foot of the terrace. On the graph paper, draw the outline of the terrace (after you've taken careful measurements), not forgetting the entrance to the terrace from the apartment, as well as any windows or other building features like chimneys, outside vents or pipes. Indicate where the drain is located and the outdoor water faucet (for your hose). Also show which way the terrace faces—north, south, east or west. The height of the parapet is also important for fencing purposes and wind control.

Now place the tracing paper over the graph paper and let your imagination take over (influenced, naturally, by your needs and the results you wish to achieve). Where would a tree look best? Where is the best view, and is this a good location for the outdoor furniture and seating arrangement? From which direction does the wind come? Is fencing needed to tame it?

Go over the list of plant categories (see charts on pages 87–99) and note how many you can use. Start doodling on the tracing paper and putting down your ideas. At first, you'll have far too much and you'll probably forget to draw them in proportion. To help you visualize as you draw, go to your local nursery and take a tape measure, along with a pad and pencil. Measure the height of a few trees and shrubs that appeal to you, and their overall circumference at maturity (don't measure the smaller and younger plants that you plan to buy—ask to see mature versions of them and measure *those* because that's how they'll look in a few years). Take measurements of planters and containers. Not only will you have all these important facts in hand, but you'll be able to *visualize* them when you get back to your terrace and start drawing the plan. Containers and boxes come in so many sizes, not to mention those made-to-order, that listing their dimensions would be fruitless. Take the measurements of what *you* want to buy, based on what is available in your locality and the cost. Get to *know* the plants and have pictures of them firmly in your head, and you'll find the paper planning fun to do.

You know how much space you have to fill in your terrace. Don't furnish every inch of it. You need room to move around, push a chair back, wield a broom, drag a hose from plant to plant. Restraint is required in order to do an editing job on your desires. Measure some of your indoor furniture to get an idea of the space outdoor furniture will take on your terrace. A straight-back chair takes the same amount of room no matter what its style (about two feet wide and fifteen inches deep); figure a thirty-six-inch–diameter round table if you want to seat four people around it for meals, and five feet is the minimum for a chaise longue if you like to lie flat while sunning. Keep in mind that an awning cuts down on the amount of sun and light when you select plants, so save the shade-loving ones for the area under the awning.

Sketch in the biggest items first: trees, then large shrubs, small shrubs, flowers, dining table, chairs, small tables and so forth. After you have the essentials in, *as they relate to your specific needs,* add (if there's still room) little luxuries—decorative touches such as statuary, fountain, a bench, a pool.

Construction work is done first when the terrace is bare, to allow room for workers to do their job. This includes the installation of fencing, awning and built-in planters, as well as any repair work to existing floor or existing planters. Once these items are out of the way, you'll have a far better picture of what your terrace looks like. It will start to take form as you bring in the "big tree" and the other plants. If lots of comfortable furniture is important to you and plants are merely a backdrop, buy the furniture first and see how much room you have left for planters and plants. (This is where putting it down on paper pays off. You might find out that you have room *only* for furniture as you've planned it, plus some top-of-the-parapet flower boxes. At least you'll know beforehand, and that's the whole point.)

A plan is needed before you start making a shopping list, since the latter will be based on what the former indicates. If it's too much for you to spend all at once, simply keep the list for future reference and buy only those items that will bring you joy in the current year. Settle for half the plants and a few pieces of furniture the first year, adding more the next, and so on. *It's important to have enough of each to start enjoying your terrace the first summer you have it.* This gives you the enthusiasm and motivation needed for going through with your initial plan. It may also change your mind about priorities and give you time to make necessary alterations to your plan. As an example, you may find that caring for the few plants you have now is about all you can handle, so you switch your initial plan for more plants to a pool with a vine backing it, or statuary or a fountain, or simply more furniture.

Long, narrow terraces are the most difficult to plan. The objective is to prevent them from looking like bowling alleys. This is done by breaking up the long space with groupings of containers, a chair and small table, a large urn, hanging baskets against a wall covered with ivy, etc. With the smaller balcony, as much off-the-ground planting as possible is required to allow room for the minimum two chairs and small table. It's best not to overwhelm such a small space with a large shrub or even a small tree. It would be out of proportion, leaving room for nothing else. Plants can be tall at either end of the balcony, but must be airy and slender in growth habit. Hanging baskets, wall containers and window boxes attached firmly to the parapet will hold enough flowers to add color and gaiety. But check with building and city authorities regarding boxes secured to the top of the parapet. Some cities won't allow you to hang them on the outside of the railing or even on top of it, no matter how securely tied they are. In this case, the boxes must be within the *inside* perimeter of the balcony.

21. SUMMERING HOUSE PLANTS

Because it's sheltered and out of reach of the scorching sun, the backyard is a far better place to summer house plants than is the terrace. The wind and intense heat of the average terrace take a heavy toll on plants that are babied all winter long indoors, away from drafts and other extremes of climate. Even the sun-loving plants can't be placed outdoors all day in full summer sun—except for cacti and succulents. If you have an awning, an ideal place for house plants is beneath it. Group them on a wicker or wrought-iron table if the area is not too windy. If you have little shelter from the wind, it's best to place the plants on the floor. At least, if they fall over, they won't come to as much harm as they would if they toppled from a table.

Furniture acts as a windbreak, so that plants grouped near it have better protection than if you were to put them in an exposed location. Against the building wall is another area that is fairly sheltered, as would also be the space between tubs of shrubs. A charming and safe display of house plants can be made with a large square or round ornamental planter, filled with sphagnum moss. Plunge the pots of house plants in it, keeping the moss damp at all times. Put more moss on the surface of the pots, and this makes an attractive display while the plants stay cool and moist. If the container is on casters, it can be moved about the terrace in case of heavy rain or sudden storms.

The culture that your house plants require indoors will be the same once they're outdoors. Shade-loving plants will still want shade and the sun-loving ones will welcome sun—although not too much, because the sun is intensified enormously on an open terrace. Specimen plants that are a part of your interior decoration are best left indoors. They're too costly an investment for you to gamble on the elements. It would take only one swift gust of wind or a downpour to do irreparable damage. Large plants are difficult to move anyway, but since most are among the exotic, low-light-requirement species, they're happiest indoors.

When the time comes to take your house plants back indoors, take advantage of the space on the terrace to do any repotting that may be necessary. Check to see if roots are coming out of the bottom drainage hole. If in doubt, gently knock the plant out of the pot and see if the roots are tightly wound in a knot with almost all the soil gone. Such plants must be repotted to a next-size-larger pot, or divided if you want additional plants to keep or give away. Prune back plants that have grown leggy during the summer, and check for bugs. A bath of soapy water is a good precaution. Rinse leaves gently and you're all set until the following summer. You'll know soon enough which plants thrived when placed outdoors and which ones obviously didn't like it one bit. Make a note of this and leave the unhappy ones indoors next year.

22. SOIL AND FERTILIZERS

All the soil for terrace planting has to be "imported." The backyard garden may not have very good soil, but at least there is a supply to start with. It can be worked thoroughly, with the necessary ingredients added to make it better. Even if fresh topsoil is purchased, there is still the subsoil to form a base—but high in the sky, *everything* has to be brought in. It can be, of course, that the previous owners of the terrace have left you a good supply of soil in the built-in planters, or have left containers filled with soil. In this case, as with the backyard, it's merely a matter of enriching the soil, preparing it in such a way that the plants will have a good start or, if plants are already established on your terrace, of giving them a top dressing of fresh soil and fertilizer.

Terrace soil dries out much faster than the backyard variety. This is because the sun is so much more intense and the air circulation is far greater due to the wind. For this reason, the soil in containers and planters has to be richer. It should have more peat moss than would normally be required in a regular garden, because this material retains moisture, conditions the soil and makes it loose and airy.

A good all-purpose soil mixture is one composed of four parts rich topsoil, one part peat moss, one part perlite and a handful of bone meal for every pailful of the mixture. Mix it all very thoroughly on a large plastic sheet spread out on the terrace. For acid-loving plants (such as broad-leaved evergreens), double the amount of peat moss and substitute dehydrated cow manure for the bone meal. For plants that love lime (not many will fall into this category, but herbs are one example), skip the peat moss altogether, double the perlite and add a handful of lime when you add the bone meal.

Buy the best grade of topsoil that is available, but if you have any doubts about its quality (it should look and feel rich), buy a bag of humus and incorporate it into the topsoil until it looks the way you want it. Terrace gardening is one area where you can err on the side of overdoing it when it comes to having rich soil. If drainage is good, rainwater will leach out the vital nutrients in the soil pretty quickly—unlike ground-level gardening, where tall buildings and trees shield the soil to a far greater degree.

Bone meal and dehydrated cow manure are both slow-acting, gentle organic fertilizers and are good to add when you originally make your soil mixture, because they propel the plants to active growth right away. Addition of a complete chemical fertilizer like 5-10-5 a year later is a good idea, when plant growth starts in the spring. Chemical fertilizers are expensive and are being channeled to underdeveloped countries for vital food cultivation, but constant enriching of the soil can be achieved nevertheless by the "black gold" of your own compost pile (see chapter 30).

The mixtures described are for those gardeners starting from scratch. If you already have available soil—dry and poor though it may be—you can upgrade it easily. In the case of built-in masonry beds, work some pure humus into the soil, as well as peat moss and bone meal or dehydrated cow manure. Mix it in as thoroughly as you can, using a cultivator (see chapter 26) to make the job easier. The soil should be loose, friable and sufficiently dark in color to denote its richness. Add perlite if the soil feels like mud when you scoop up a handful.

Your local nursery will supply you with all these ingredients in convenient quantity and easy-to-handle plastic bags. Don't go by the size of the bag, but by its weight. You'll be amazed when you pick up the perlite. It's featherweight . . . but not so the limestone!

Where there is very little planting, as on a balcony, start with a fresh soil mixture in the window boxes instead of carrying over the previous tenant's soil (and possible bugs). If you wish to follow a regular fertilizing routine, the time to do it is from late May to September, every two or three weeks. However, don't fertilize shrubs and woody plants after August, as the soft new growth that is stimulated will be winter-killed. Use a liquid fertilizer, as it's more convenient, although more expensive than the solid variety— so little is needed. Of the solid types of fertilizers, granular is best, as it's easy to spread (the powdered kind blows away).

The three digits on the fertilizer bag represent the percentage of nitrogen, phosphorus and potash. Example: 20-20-10 (good for lawns) means the bag holds 20 percent nitrogen, 20 percent phosphorus and 10 percent potash—the rest is made up of fillers. Nitrogen is good for the stems and leaves of the plant, while phosphorus is beneficial to every phase of plant growth. Potash makes plants vigorous and disease-resistant. There are many formulas on the market, some for specific plants only. The latter are usually a waste of money unless you happen to have a very large number of one kind of plant, such as roses.

It pays off in the long run to take the time and trouble to mix good soil in planters and containers. Plants will be healthier, will bloom more and will derive the strength needed to fight strong winds, pollution and other high-rise gardening hazards. Considering the cost of plants these days, it seems wise to ensure their longevity by growing them in the best possible soil. Once this is done, they'll need only occasional booster shots of fertilizers, far less than would be the case if they were planted in poor, deficient soil.

There is no use denying that terrace gardeners are tied down to a rigid watering schedule, since their soil dries out considerably faster than that of their backyard-gardening friends. However, help has arrived. The wonders of modern science have come up with a product that should be of great help to all gardeners, but especially to those whose gardens consist of containers or shallow beds. Union Carbide Corporation has developed a soil amendment called Viterra Hydrogel, previously available only to commercial growers. This material holds up to twenty-five times its own weight in water. It holds water in the root zone, making it available to the plant as needed—thereby lengthening the time plants can go without watering and still remain strong and healthy. Seed flats and seedlings which need a steady amount of moisture particularly benefit when this material is added to their soil mixture, as do hanging baskets, which dry out faster than any other form of gardening.

Thoroughly mix Viterra Hydrogel into your soil at the rate of two and three-fourths cups per bushel of soil. For already potted plants, use the following rates:

One heaping half-teaspoon for each three-inch pot
One and one-half heaping teaspoons for each four-inch pot
Two heaping teaspoons for each five-inch pot
Four heaping teaspoons for each six-inch pot

Viterra can also be used for indoor house-plant soil—a blessing for frequent travelers with guilt feelings about their neglected plants. Transplant shock is also radically reduced because roots grow into the tiny granules which are small water reservoirs, and which then remain with the transplant. This is good to remember when planting tomatoes or peppers. Before transplanting them to their new location, add some Viterra to the soil. If it's not available locally, Burpee's carries the product in its catalog (see chapter 35). If, for reasons of weight, you are restricted to making your own artificial soil mixture, see page 135 for instructions. For small quantities, you can mix two parts of prepared Jiffy Mix with one part of perlite or vermiculite.

23. MULCHES

High-rise gardens need mulching even more than do backyard gardens, and the latter certainly require it (see chapter 12). The reasons are the same, but intensified. Because of excessive winds and sun, plants dry out much faster on terraces, and a good mulch applied several inches thick delays the drying process. It not only retains moisture longer in the soil, but also keeps roots cool and prevents weeds. Some mulches add nutrients to the soil as they break down slowly, helping to maintain the friable, loose texture of the soil. Soil can easily become hard and compacted, depriving the roots of necessary oxygen. A mulch will prevent a heavy rain from compacting the soil. And as if all this weren't enough, a mulch is attractive, unifying the garden, giving the flower beds and large planters a "finished" look.

Because of high winds, select a mulch that will not blow away easily (see chapter 12 for a variety of mulches available). If finely shredded bark is chosen (it's usually the number-one choice), cover it with a layer of the larger-sized nuggets to keep it down in a windstorm. Ornamental stones are another good choice, and they come in so many different sizes and types that one will certainly be suitable for your garden. I would stay away from leaves and lightweight hulls of any sort, unless your terrace is unusually well-sheltered from the wind.

To be effective, a mulch should be from three to four inches thick. Expect a slight loss each year because some will blow away, wash off in rain, or disintegrate into the soil (stones sometimes sink under the surface of the soil). Adding a bit of fresh mulch each year will keep it at the desired depth.

A mulch can be applied any time of the year, but the best time is obviously in late spring when you're finished with planting. Water the plants thoroughly and cover large containers and flower beds with a thick layer of mulch. Thereafter, until winter, water as you normally would; the water will go through the mulch and into the roots (as will a liquid fertilizer), but the moisture will not escape as rapidly as it would without that layer of mulch.

Once a permanent mulch is applied, every time you want to put in a new plant simply push the mulch aside, stick the plant in the soil and spread the mulch back around the plant. Nothing much can be done about the looks of a bare terrace in the winter, but having the empty beds covered neatly by an attractive mulch helps to improve the appearance.

24. PREPARING FOR WINTER AND FOR SPRING

Harsh winds, more than cold weather, kill plants during the winter months. This applies only to evergreens, since they're the only ones around at that time. Annuals are dead, and perennials and other deciduous plants are dormant. Evergreen shrubs and trees, however, can be dehydrated and suffer severe damage.

The most sensible preventive step is to stick with wind-hardy specimens. The next is to take a few precautions. Keep watering evergreens deeply right into winter and during the winter months occasionally, whenever you're sure the temperature will not dip below freezing. Make sure the mulch is good and thick, *not* to keep the roots of plants warm but to keep the soil from heaving during the warmer days in mid-winter when roots can be exposed by wide cracks in the soil. The mulch keeps an even, cold temperature, preventing any such heaving.

Antidessicant sprays have now replaced the burlap windscreens as a means of preventing water loss caused by strong winds. Sprays such as Wilt-pruf and others form a protective coating over the leaves, sealing the pores and preventing moisture from escaping. Spray evergreens thoroughly with this mixture (it comes in aerosol form for small jobs, or you can mix your own if you have many trees and shrubs to spray) in late fall/early winter and then again in mid-winter—an early spring dose is also helpful. The coating eventually disappears on its own later in the spring. But you may have to resort to both the spray and the burlap windscreen if yours is an unusually windy terrace, especially for container plants, as these are more vulnerable to the elements.

After a heavy snowfall, upright spreading shrubs can have branches broken if they are spread apart under the excess weight. To prevent this, secure the branches together with strong twine or rope. Use a broom to shake snow from branches of trees and shrubs, but do this very gently. With smaller plants use your hand. With ice, however, it's best to leave it alone and let it melt on its own. Trying to break it off the branches will only increase the damage and watering the plant will obviously add still more if the temperature is below freezing.

Cleaning up the terrace in early spring is a quick job. Of course, this is true only if in late fall a cleanup of dead annuals and other plants was done in preparation for winter. The most important job, after winter is definitely over, is to check all plants for damage from wind or snow. Torn branches should be pruned quickly. Inspect the year-round mulch to see if it needs replenishing to keep it at the desired three- to four-inch depth. Put away windscreens and untie branches. Gradually remove the small mounds of soil placed at the bases of rose bushes to help them through the winter.

Trim dead ends of vines and secure them to walls if they have been torn away. Check ground covers and clip off dead tips. Now is the time to do repair work on containers, cracks in flooring, broken brackets for hanging baskets, torn awnings and anything else that needs fixing. Outdoor furniture may need a coat of paint. Fencing should also be examined because a small job done now will prevent a much bigger expense later on. Sweep the terrace clean and finish off with a good hosing of flooring and plants. Everything should be clean and sparkling, ready for spring planting and a new outdoor season.

What to Plant Where

TREES

Important Note: Height and spread of trees at maturity are not given because these differ with each variety. One kind of tree may come in several varieties, each with its own special growth habit. Also, trees grown in containers or terrace beds have their roots restricted and automatically never reach their full height. Exposure and climate affect growth of trees. When buying the tree, inquire about its ultimate height and width. This is most important to remember.

Botanical Name	Common Name	Deciduous	Evergreen	Blooming Season	Hardiness Zone (southward)	For Backyards Only	For Terraces Only	Good Anywhere	
Acer palmatum	Japanese Maple	X			4	X			Graceful and delicate foliage. Is best used as a specimen tree. Don't use sprays on it. Needs winter protection if container-grown.
Ailanthus altissima	Tree-of-Heaven	X			4			X	One of the most pollution-resistant trees. Buy only the female varieties (odor of male flowers is unpleasant).
Albizzia julibrissin	Silktree	X		summer	6			X	Very attractive. Will not survive cold winters without protection. Variety *rosea* now called "Ernest Wilson" is hardier, more compact and has deeper pink flowers; can be grown from zone 5 southward.
Betula papyrifera	Canoe or Paper Birch	X			5 northward to Arctic	X			All birches are short-lived but so beautiful that they should be included whenever possible; stunning teamed with evergreens for contrast. *B. pendula* is a smaller variety, has drooping branches and is more frequently seen in cities; can be grown from zone 3 southward.
Carpinus betulus columnaris	European Hornbeam	X			4			X	Slender, pyramidal tree. Good for hedges. Slow grower. Birch-like leaves. Bears catkins and nutlets that attract birds.
Cornus florida	Flowering Dogwood	X		spring	5	X			Likes acid soil and part shade. White flowers and berries in the fall. Variety *rubra* has pink flowers.
Cornus mas	Cornelian Cherry	X		spring	4	X			Small tree, yellow flowers, scarlet fruit. More smoke-resistant and city-enduring than Dogwood.
Crataegus oxyacantha	English Hawthorn	X		early summer	4			X	*C. lavallei* and *C. phaenopyrum* are also good for containers. White flowers but some varieties are pink or red. Bright fruit. Some have columnar habit, others droop.
Elaeagnus angustifolia	Russian Olive	X		early summer	3		X		Not very showy flowers but handsome, willowy, silver foliage. Likes dry areas. *E. multiflora* is very smoke- and wind-resistant. These trees are excellent windbreaks.
Ginkgo biloba	Maidenhair Tree	X			5 northward			X	Use male plant only. Withstands wind well. Some varieties are as narrow and straight as columns, others spread wide.
Gleditsia triacanthos	Honey Locust	X			4		X		Airy foliage does not give deep shade. Some varieties are thornless (buy those if you can) and some are very slender. Likes alkaline soil. Tolerates sun, smoke and drought.

TREES

Botanical name	Common name		Flowering			Comments
Juniperus virginiana	Red Cedar	X		2	X	Pyramid shape and fragrant foliage. Excellent as background or screening.
Magnolia soulangeana	Saucer Magnolia	X	spring	3		Spectacular flower show. Comes in several varieties. For locations in zone 7 southward, *M. grandiflora* will grow well in large containers.
Malus floribunda	Japanese Flowering Crab-Apple	X	spring	4	X	Likes alkaline soil. A great show of flowers in spring and bright fruit in the fall. Many other varieties available. Choose the smaller ones for terraces.
Olea europaea	Common Olive	X		7		Good for container-growing in California and similar warm climates.
Phyllostachys aurea	Golden Bamboo	X		6		Most bamboos make good container plants for warm climates. They require lots of water.
Picea abies	Norway Spruce	X		3	X	Also *P. glauca albertiana*, "Alberta Spruce." Look for the many dwarf varieties in all the spruces. They only reach one- to two-feet-high, even when mature.
Pinus mugo mughus	Dwarf Swiss Mountain Pine	X		3	X	Shrubby, low, prostrate form. Terrific used in mass planting. Very hardy and attractive.
Pinus nigra	Austrian Pine	X		4	X	Pyramidal shape. Several varieties available. All are especially well-suited to cities.
Pinus strobus	White Pine	X		3	X	One of the most beautiful of evergreens. Likes acid soil, but not too much moisture. Great for screening.
Pinus sylvestris	Scots Pine	X		3	X	Likes wind, so use as a windbreak. Very picturesque tree. Tolerates any soil.
Pinus thunbergi	Japanese Black Pine	X		4	X	When it comes to surviving under the fiercest wind conditions, none can top this tree. If everything you've tried on your windy terrace has died, get this pine before giving up.
Platanus acerifolia	London Planetree	X		4	X	One of the most dirt- smoke- soot-resistant of all trees, which is why it's so popular in large cities.
Prunus glandulosa	Flowering Almond	X	spring	4	X	Several varieties with pink or white flowers. It's not a true almond tree, but it's treasured for its beautiful flowers. *P. triloba* in the variety *florepleno* is also a beauty.
Prunus subhirtella	Japanese Flowering Cherry	X	spring	4	X	A rare delight of a tree for beautiful flower display. The *pendula* variety has graceful, drooping branches, superb as a specimen. For a second show of flowers in the fall, try *P. subhirtella autumnalis*.
Quercus palustris	Pin Oak	X		4	X	Fast-growing tree that likes acid soil. Some varieties are narrower and more upright than others so choose what is most suitable for your space.
Salix alba	White Willow	X		3	X	There's also *S. babylonica*, "Weeping Willow." All willows are graceful-looking, but need much water and have brittle branches.
Sophora japonica	Japanese Pagoda Tree	X	summer	4	X	Showy flowers, handsome round-headed tree. Variety *pendula* has sweeping branches. Tolerates dry soil.
Tsuga canadensis	Canada (common) Hemlock	X		3	X	Excellent for screening or as a hedge, but needs plenty of room. Dwarf variety *compacta* has many uses, as has the *pendula* variety which is low, broad, with pendulous branches.

SHRUBS

Botanical Name	Common Name	Deciduous	Evergreen	Blooming Season	Hardiness Zone (southward)	For Backyards Only	For Terraces Only	Good Anywhere	
Abelia grandiflora	Glossy Abelia	X		summer	6	X			Semi-evergreen shrub with small, shiny leaves and pink or white flowers. Takes sun or light shade.
Azalea *A. hinoclegiri* *A. poukhanense* *A. rosmarinifolia*	Azalea		X	late spring	5, 6	X			There are Oriental, European, and native American species, and so many hybrids and varieties of azaleas available today, that making a complete listing is impossible. As a rule, azaleas need light shade (but enough good sun for best blooms) and a sheltered location. They require humus-rich, acid soil. Their shallow root systems need a steady supply of moisture. Best bet is to see what is available and growing well in your particular city and to stick to this variety. Species listed here are all hardy, provided they have a certain amount of protection and mulch.
Berberis thunbergi	Japanese Barberry	X		spring	4			X	Yellow flowers and red berries well into winter. Tolerates shade well. *Be. julianae* is evergreen but not as vigorous.
Buddleia davidi	Butterflybush or Summer Lilac	X		summer to frost	6		X		Needs full sun and rich soil. Has fragrant "lilac" flowers. A beautiful shrub but needs space. In hardiness zones 4 and 5, it will grow well, but may "dieback" after a severe winter; however, it grows back and blooms again the following summer.
Buxus sempervirens	Boxwood		X		5	X			No doubt one of the handsomest of hedges and tolerant of city pollution, but *not* of sun or wind. Must be given winter protection in cold areas. It has shallow roots, so don't plant or dig soil around it. Do not fertilize, but apply limestone every few years if soil is very acid. *B. suffruticosa* is a dwarf species that is excellent for use as edging of flower beds. There are many other species, including the Korean and Japanese boxwoods (*B. microphylla* and *B. microphylla koreana*) which are hardier than the English and American ones.
Calluna vulgaris	Heather	X		summer through fall	5			X	Many varieties of different heights. Excellent plant for rock gardens. Requires mixture of peat and sand in its soil. To keep bushy, trim tops every year. Provide good drainage, full sun, moisture and winter protection.
Cotoneaster divaritaca	Cotoneaster	X		spring	5			X	Good border shrub for shady spot. Small pink flowers, red berries and purple foliage in fall. *C. horizontalis* is similar to *C. divaritaca* but is low and spreads.

		X				
Deutzia gracilis	Deutzia	X	spring	4		Numerous white flowers. Variety *rosea* has pink flowers, but only for zone 5 southward. Easy to grow. *D. scabra* is a summer-blooming variety, hardy from zone 5, and comes in several varieties, including dwarf and double-flowered.
Euonymus alatus compactus	Winged Spindle-tree or Flamebush	X		4		Brilliant leaves and scarlet fruit in autumn. A compact shrub. *E. fortunei* (Wintercreeper) is an evergreen trailing vine which comes in many handsome varieties.
Forsythia	Forsythia	X	spring	3		This popular, golden-yellow flowering shrub likes sun for maximum blooms. It's also more tolerant than most shrubs of city smoke and pollution. Easy to grow and to propagate.
Hibiscus syriacus	Rose-of-Sharon	X	summer through fall	4	X	A handsome shrub bringing flowers in the garden when most needed. Many varieties available in several colors.
Hydrangea paniculata grandiflora	Peegee Hydrangea	X	summer	3	X	The hardiest and most common form of Hydrangea. Handsome but more delicate to grow is *H. macrophylla*, the type of Hydrangea seen in florists' shops. These make superb container plants, but only in zones 5 southward, unless given careful winter protection.
Hypericum moserianum	St. John's-Wort, Goldflower	X	summer	6	X	Yellow flowers. Good, small shrub in front of taller shrubs.
Ilex crenata	Japanese Holly		X	5	X	The finest and hardiest of all hollies for the city. Comes in several varieties in varying heights. Best ones are *convexa, microphylla,* and *latifolia*. The last one is great as a hedge.
Juniperus chinensis pfitzeriana	Pfitzer Juniper		X	3	X	Full sun. Tolerates, dry, windy locations making them by far your best bet for terraces in the evergreen-shrub category. Growth habit is partly upright, spreading branches. Other excellent junipers are *J. sabina* (upright) and *J. horizontalis* (creeping). All these junipers come in many varieties from dwarf to quite tall. Select the ones best suited to your needs.
Kalmia latifolia	Mountain Laurel	X	spring	4	X	Handsome, broad-leafed shrub with lovely pink flowers. Needs acid soil and part shade or sun. Not among the hardiest plants for cities, but if they like their site, they'll do well. Their beauty makes them worth a try.
Leucothoë catesbaei	Drooping Leucothoë	X	spring	4	X	Low, drooping branches with fragrant flowers and leaves that turn red-bronze in winter. A graceful shrub that adds much to the flower border. It needs plenty of moisture and humus.
Ligustrum ovalifolium	California Privet	X		4	X	Surely the most commonly used hedge plant! A semi-evergreen, it can be killed by very severe winters. *L. vulgare* (Common Privet) is hardier but does not keep its leaves as long. Both can grow anywhere from five-feet to well over fifteen. For a lower, spreading type that also blooms quite well, try *L. obtusifolium regelianum* (Regel's Privet). Do not be tempted to replace Privet with Arborvitae which admittedly is handsomer, but does not take to urban culture and environment unless you're prepared to replace it yearly.

Scientific Name	Common Name			Bloom Season	Zone		Description
Lonicera fragrantissima	Winter Honeysuckle		X	later winter, early spring	4	X	Evergreen in warm climates. Handsome foliage and fragrant flowers. Spreading branches form a round, good-looking shrub. Takes kindly to sun and wind. If you want a later blooming honeysuckle (early summer) try *L. morrowii*, hardy from zone 3.
Mahonia aquifolium	Oregon Grape		X	spring	4	X	Leaves resemble Christmas Holly, a low shrub with fragrant, yellow flowers and blue-black berries later on. Prefers shade and needs a sheltered location away from wind and excessive sun which burns the leaves. Give it winter covering.
Philadelphus lemoinei	Mock-orange		X	early summer	3	X	This is a good addition to the garden because of the very fragrant flowers on a neat, upright shrub. A hybrid, it comes in several varieties.
Pieris japonica	Andromeda		X	spring	5	X	Give it shelter from the wind and slightly acid soil and you'll have one of the handsomest shrubs available. Semi-drooping branches, whitish flowers that hang in clusters. For a more compact and lower shrub, there's *P. floribunda*.
Pyracantha coccinea lalandii	Laland Firethorn		X		5	X	In zone 4, needs to be sheltered from the wind and in a warm spot. Can take the sun. White flowers in early summer, but it's for the glorious display of orange berries in the fall that makes this shrub so well-liked. Excellent as a hedge or against a wall. "Lo Boy" is the dwarf spreading form of the same shrub.
Rhododendron wilsoni	Rhododendron		X	summer	4 to 6 only	X	A good Rhododendron in front of taller shrubs as it is low and compact. Droops over walls. Lavender-pink flowers. Needs part shade and protection. Rhododendrons like acid soil and a mulch to protect their shallow roots. For terrace gardeners who crave a Rhododendron, there is one that is unlike all others in that it tolerates dry alkaline soil in a sunny spot: *R. mucronulatum* (Korean Rhododendron), sometimes sold as *Azalea daurica*. It's covered with superb rosy-purple flowers in early spring and is deciduous.)
• *Rosa*	Rose	•	X	summer	de-pends on species	X	Roses need winter protection in severe climates. They all love the sun and some are quite tolerant of wind. As a guide, miniatures, shrub, grandifloras and climbers are good *anywhere*. Polyanthas and floribundas are best for terraces. Hybrid teas are very tricky and only for *sunny* backyards. All these roses come in many varieties, heights, growth habits, colors. Make your selection carefully based on *your* local climate and recommendations of a good nursery. Do not crowd roses with other plants. They require and deserve their own flower bed or containers. Shield them from mid-afternoon sun on south or west terraces.
Sambucus canadensis	American Elderberry		X	summer	3	X	Needs space and moist locations. Tolerates city smoke well. You can use the purple-black fruits for winemaking if you're in an early-American mood! Several varieties available including golden-leaved ones.
Spiraea vanhouttei	Spirea		X	late spring	4	X	One of the several species called Bridalwreath. A slender shrub with graceful, drooping branches and numerous white flower clusters. Needs sun and moisture. *S. bumalda*, a smaller, more compact shrub which flowers in mid-summer, comes in several varieties. All of these shrubs withstand smoke and pollution better than average.

SHRUBS

Botanical Name	Common Name	Annual	Perennial	Blooming Season	For Backyards Only	For Terraces Only	Good Anywhere	Description
Taxus baccata repandens	English Yew		5				X	The hardiest of the English yews; low, compact shrub with spreading branches. Still hardier however, from zone 4 southward (3, if protected), is the Japanese Yew, T. cuspidata and its very compact varieties, densa and nana. For use as a hedge, the tall, narrow upright T. media hicksi is very good. While some yews may do well on high terraces, they are not nearly as suitable as junipers since they do not tolerate open, wind-swept locations. Sheltered terraces on lower floors are o.k., however. Otherwise, be prepared to give them good winter protection.
Viburnum	Viburnum		4	late spring			X	There are many species of this superb shrub, some of which are evergreen. Attractive flowers, brilliant flowers, brilliant fall foliage and bluish or red berries. Good species to choose from: V. opulus nanum (withstands pollution well), V. dilatatum, V. prunifolium, V. tomentosum.
Weigela florida	Weigela		4	late spring	X			Many varieties of this popular shrub. Showy flowers can be rose-pink, white or dark pink. An easy shrub to grow.

ANNUALS AND PERENNIALS

Note: In warm climates, some annuals are perennials. So many varieties are now available, ranging from dwarf to very tall (such as marigolds) that giving exact height is impossible. Check marker in pot for height at maturity or ask nurseryman. As a rule, shade-loving plants are for backyards and sun-loving ones for terraces, but some are happy anywhere. Bulbs are included in this listing.

Botanical Name	Common Name	Annual	Perennial	Blooming Season	For Backyards Only	For Terraces Only	Good Anywhere	Description
Achillea	Yarrow		X	summer		X		Thrives on sun. Hardy. Heavy bloomer (white, pink or yellow flowers, although yellow most popular). Many species of varying heights and growth habits. Some excellent ones for rock gardens.
Adiantum pedatum	Maidenhair Fern		X		X			Ferns are a handsome addition to the moist and shady backyard. There are so many species to choose from. The Cinnamon fern and the Christmas fern are two popular ones.
Alyssum saxatile	Golden-tuft		X	spring		X		Wide, bushy and spreads rapidly. Dwarf plant with golden-yellow flowers. Several varieties. Needs full sun.
Arisaema triphyllum	Jack-in-the-Pulpit		X	spring	X			A wildflower garden is possible if your backyard is moist and shady. Add lots of leafmold to the soil and keep a mulch on at all times. (Pine needles and leaves are great.) Combine ferns, violets, Snakeroot, Trillium, Hepatica, Troutlily. You may even get the yellow Lady's Slipper to thrive! Many other wildflowers to choose from.

Botanical Name	Common Name		Season			Notes
Asclepias tuberosa	Butterfly-weed	X	summer			Likes dry, sandy soil, showy, bright orange flowers. Can grow to three-feet-tall.
Aster	Michaelmas Daisy	X	fall			Provides color in the garden when most needed, in late summer and fall. Many varieties in varying heights and colors. Give it rich, moist soil and divide clumps annually for best results.
Begonia semperflorens	Wax Begonia	X	summer		X	It may be the most common and ordinary type of Begonia, but it's at home anywhere, although part shade is its ideal location. It's best used as an edging or border plant, all of one color, or alternating two at the most. It needs plenty of moisture, but other than that is not in the least demanding. Buy grown, potted plants for quick and best results. Dig up a few before frost, pot them, cut them back and bring them indoors for winter pleasure. Many colors and varieties.
Bellis perennis	English Daisy	X	spring	X		Will do well in partial shade. Mass plants together for best effect. Also good in window boxes. Under six-inches-high.
Browallia speciosa major	Browallia	X	summer			Lovely blue flowers. Compact plant under two-feet-high.
Centaurea cyanus	Cornflower or Bachelors-Button	X	summer			Pale blue flowers, sprawling growth habit. Several varieties in other colors. Doesn't mind being crowded.
Chrysanthemum	Chrysanthemum	X	fall			So many varieties, but it's best to stick with the cushion variety, for its compact habit, but keep pinching the terminal shoots until end of July. Use the cascade variety for large containers or over a low wall. Divide plants yearly for maximum blooms.
Coleus blumei	Coleus	X			X	Likes sun or shade. Has blue-purple flower spikes, but is grown for its brilliant foliage of many hues. Keep pinching plant to keep it bushy. Many people snip off flower buds to concentrate plant's energy into foliage growth. Colors are more intense if plant is in the sun. Do not set out plants until all danger of frost is well past. If grown on a terrace, give it a sheltered spot and keep moist.
Convallaria majalis	Lily-of-the-Valley	X	spring	X		For shady, woodsy areas. Can make a lovely ground cover if allowed to roam. Fragrant white flowers.
Coreopsis grandiflora	Tickseed	X	summer			Yellow flowers. Plant not over two-feet-high. Annual species are also available.
Dahlia	Dahlia	X	summer			The dwarf varieties are the best and easiest to care for on a terrace. Mass the plants for a dramatic show of colors. These are grown from bulbs planted in spring or bought already growing and blooming. Many colors available.
Dianthus plumarius	Cottage Pink	X	spring			Many varieties. Likes sandy soil. Fragrant flowers in several colors, some variegated. Dig up and divide every three years for best results and blooming.

ANNUALS AND PERENNIALS

Botanical Name	Common Name		Season			Description
Dicentra spectabilis	Bleeding Heart	X	spring			Easily grown, has showy clusters of rose or red flowers. Delightful in a naturalistic setting. For a really woody area, *D. eximia* is most appealing.
Gaillardia aristata	Blanketflower		summer	X		Showy orange-red flowers. Hardy plant two- to three-feet-high. Give it full sun. There are several annual species as well that are very nice and also have daisy-like flowers.
Gladiolus	Gladiolus	X	summer	X		Grown from corms in species and varieties so numerous that it boggles the mind! They are formal-looking plants and best placed in rows against a fence or wall or in clumps in between evergreens, but they need full sun and plenty of water.
Hemerocallis	Daylily	X	summer		X	One of my favorite of all plant families. A few plants make a spectacular show. Many varieties which come in varying sizes and colors and time of bloom. Sun or shade. Needs room. Divide every few years.
Herbs	Herbs	X		X	X	Some herbs are annual (Basil, Parsley, Dill, Borage); others are perennial (Chives, Marjoram, Mint, Rosemary, Sage, Tarragon, Thyme). Most will grow well anywhere if given plenty of sun and light soil. Buy started plants whenever possible.
Heuchera sanguinea	Coralbells	X	summer			Red bell-shaped flowers. Several varieties. Good for the partly shaded border.
Hibiscus moscheutos	Rosemallow	X	summer	X		Fabulous flowers! (Colors depend on variety.) A showy, dramatic plant that should be in its own container. Give it rich soil with plenty of humus and keep moist. A showpiece when in bloom.
Hosta	Plantain-Lily, Funkia	X	summer	X		Invaluable plants for the shady, moist garden, although they do well in sun as well as long as they are kept moist. Many species and varieties, all of which have handsome foliage. Size of plant varies with species. Flowers are tall spikes, white or light purple, sometimes fragrant. Group at least three for a bold effect in the garden. The smaller species are great as edging. Easily divided to get more plants.
Hyacinthus	Hyacinth	X	spring		X	Fragrant and beautiful spring bulbs. Must have sun. Best to treat as an annual if you want maximum bloom. Because they are rather formal-looking, plant them in tubs surrounded with ivy or group them in clumps in the flower border. Avoid planting in rows.
Iberis sempervirens	Candytuft	X	spring, early summer	X		Grows in low, compact clumps which makes it great as an edging plant. Foliage stays evergreen in most sections of the county. Flowers are white and can often be made to bloom again later in the summer if the plant is clipped back. Plants can easily be divided to make more for your border. Keep plant moist.
Impatiens sultani	Impatiens, Patience Plant	X	summer			A superb plant for the shady garden. Will also do well in partly sunny spots, but will not take full sun. Blooms from early summer until frost, non-stop. Many varieties available in varying colors. Some attain shrub-like proportions. Don't allow to get dry. Could be grown on a terrace but only if put in a sheltered shady spot.

Iris sibirica	Siberian Iris	early summer	X		Likes sun but a moist soil which makes it suitable for the backyard. For terraces, stick with the bearded species as they thrive on hot sun and can tolerate dry soil. *I. pumila* is a dwarf species, very good for rock gardens anywhere. Blooming time depends on species and varieties as does height.
Lantana	Lantana	summer	X	X	Must have full sun and tolerates dry soil very well making it ideal for terraces. Doesn't stop blooming all-summerlong. A perennial in warm climates. Can reach shrub-like size, making it suitable for tub culture. There's a trailing species that is popular for hanging baskets or as a gound cover. A very fine plant well worth trying.
Lobelia cardinalis	Cardinal-flower	summer	X	X	Ideal for shady, moist places, although it will tolerate part sun if soil is moist. Tall, showy, scarlet flower spikes. Plant in back of the border because it can reach five-feet if it's really happy.
Lobelia erinus	Lobelia	summer	X	X	Low edging plant, especially the variety *compacta*. Blue flowers, but also available in a white variety. The trailing variety is the one used for hanging baskets.
Narcissus	Daffodil	spring	X	X	Nothing quite makes you feel spring has finally arrived as seeing a few clumps of daffodils gaily popping out of the ground. They're the only spring bulbs you don't have to treat as annuals to get a good show out of them for a few years. Plant them in informal groups and don't cut off the foliage when it turns brown. Let it die down naturally for flowers the following year. Sun or part shade. Many varieties available but stick with the hardy weatherproof ones that can take wind and rain without damage.
Nicotiana alata grandiflora	Flowering Tobacco	summer	X	X	A tall erect plant grown chiefly for its lovely and fabulously fragrant white flowers which bloom all summer. Best in the sun, but does tolerate part shade nicely. Keep moist during hot spells. Plant a few in pots close to the place you sit in the evening so you can fully enjoy the fragrance.
Pelargonium hortorum	Geranium	spring through fall	X	X	Sun or partial shade, but dislikes intense heat, so give it a sheltered spot on an open rooftop. Make wonderful container plants as they like being slightly pot-bound and dry soil. For this reason, keep them in the pot when you plant them in the flower border; bury pot in the ground. You'll get more flowers and less foliage. The Ivy Geranium is excellent for hanging baskets and likes more moisture.
Petunia hybrida	Petunia	summer	X	X	Fragrant, delightful flowers. Sun or part shade. Needs protection however, as its weak stems break easily in a very high wind or heavy rain, although new varieties are being brought out which claim greater hardiness. Petunias make great window-box and hanging-basket plants in the cascading varieties. Although they're popular bedding plants, I personally prefer them in pots or tubs. Available in many forms, sizes and colors. The dwarf, bushy varieties are best for bedding.

ANNUALS AND PERENNIALS

Botanical name	Common name			Blooming time		Remarks
Phlox subulata	Moss Pink		X	spring	X	Needs sun. Wide, bushy plant that spreads rapidly. Excellent for the rock garden. Blue, pink or red flowers. Needs no special care. It's low enough to make a mat-like ground cover. Pretty when allowed to creep over the edge of a brick border.
Polianthes tuberosa	Tuberose		X	summer		Intensely fragrant flowering bulb with waxy-white blooms. Plant the tuber in late spring and keep well-watered. Lift tubers in fall and store dry in temperature around 60 degrees.
Portulaca	Purslane	X	X	summer		A trailing, low, fleshy-stemmed plant that thrives on hot sun and dry soil. Ideal for rock gardens. Has very gay, pretty flowers in different colors depending on varieties.
Primula polyantha	Primrose		X	spring	X	A delight for the moist, shady backyard. Flowers in many colors. A handsome hybrid and the easiet of all primroses to grow. Other species bloom earlier or later, but all need a moist soil and a shady site, especially during summer.
Pulmonaria angustifolia	Lungwort		X	spring	X	Low-growing plant grown mainly for its attractive foliage. Will do well in ordinary soil but needs shade. Easily propagated by division. An attractive addition to a naturalistic garden.
Rudbeckia hirta	Black-eyed Susan	X	X	Summer		This species often turns into a perennial. Cheerful golden-yellow flowers with brown centers. Can grow to three-feet-high. Prefers full sun, but tolerates light shade. Not to be confused with the vine of the same name.
Sedum spectabile	Stonecrop, Liveforever	X	X	depends on species		*S. spectabile* is a tallish, upright species with pink flowers in late summer. Very hearty, thrives anywhere although it prefers sun. The trailing sedums, such as *S. sieboldi* and *S. spurium* among many others, are best kept for terrace culture as they require full sun and dry soil. Perfect for the rockery. *S. acre* will take over completely forming a low, moss-like carpet. A good ground cover for dry spots, if you can control it!
Sempervivum tectorum	Hen-and-Chicks	X	X	early summer		A must for the rock garden. Practically nothing can kill it. Needs full sun and dry soil. Great to fill in cracks and also very effective in large strawberry jars. Many species to choose from. Once planted, forget about them! Made-to-order for the terrace gardener.
Tagetes	Marigold	X	X	summer through fall		The backbone of the annual flower bed. So many varieties in all different heights. Needs sun. Dwarf species are great edging, a border or in front of taller marigolds. They keep blooming until frost. The lemon-yellow varieties combined with the bright orange one or the deeper burnt-orange mixed-types make for a spectacular design.
Tulipa	Tulip	X	X	spring		Treat as an annual if you want good flowers. Plant in containers or in clumps in the flower bed. Avoid row-like planting unless you want a very formal, stiff design. Many species. varieties, colors. Needs sun. Buy top-quality bulbs.

Botanical Name	Common Name				Description
Viola odorata	Sweet Violet	X	spring	X	For the shady spots in the backyard garden, especially the naturalistic, woody type. Spreads rapidly. Fragrant flowers.
Yucca filamentosa	Adams-needle	X	late summer	X	For a dramatic tub specimen, this bold desert plant is tough to beat! Spectacular sword-like foliage, with handsome flower show. Several species available that are suitable for different parts of the country. Can be planted directly in the ground, but in this case, combine with rock-garden design and plants to keep the exotic, desert "mood."
Zinnia	Zinnia		summer	X	Needs sun. A reliable, colorful annual that is easy to grow. Comes in many varieties, colors and heights. Dwarf types are good as edging or in pots.

GROUND COVERS AND VINES

Any plant that creeps, trails or spreads rapidly can be used and considered a ground cover. For city gardens, they should be low plants to fit into the scale of the overall design. They can be allowed to roam unchecked if absolutely no maintenance is to be given the garden. Vines take up little of the precious ground space, yet can cover much vertically and add great charm. Some are suitable for window boxes, as are some of the ground covers. Remember that many vines can hang down as well as climb up, so use your imagination!

Botanical Name	Common Name	Deciduous	Evergreen	Hardiness Zone (southward)	Ground Cover Only	Vine Only	Ground Cover and/or Vine	For Backyards Only	For Terraces Only	Good anywhere	Description
Actinidia arguta	Taravine	X		3			X	X			A high-climbing, woody vine with shiny leaves and whitish flowers in summer. Part shade or sun. A quick grower to cover arbors or trellises. Perennial.
Ajuga	Bugleweed	X		5	X			X			Really more of a semi-evergreen. Sun or shade. Tall blue, white or pink flower spines in late spring. Spreads quickly. Perennial.

GROUND COVERS AND VINES

Botanical Name	Common Name				Zone			Description
Akebia quinata	Five-leaf Akebia	X	X		4		X	A very good low-growing vine with handsome foliage and tiny deep-pink flowers. It's a delicate, slender vine, but needs pruning to prevent it from spreading all over the ground, unless you wish to use it as a ground cover and have plenty of room for it. Good for a low wall. Perennial.
Calonyction aculeatum	Moonflower	X	X		3		X	A perennial in zones 9 southward, an annual in other zones. Because its flowers open only in the evening, it's frequently planted as a companion to Morning-glory. Tolerates partial shade. Large, fragrant flowers. Withstands city pollution very well.
Campsis radicans	Trumpet-Vine	X	X		4		X	Very tolerant of city pollution. A rampant grower, tough and hard to keep within bounds, so give it plenty of room. Brilliant orange-red flowers in late summer. Perennial.
Clematis paniculata	Japanese Clematis	X	X		3		X	For success, remember that Clematis likes lime in the soil, its roots cool and moist, and its "head" in the sun. Small, fragrant, white flowers in the fall. Needs support to climb. The fancy hybrids are more spectacular but harder to grow. Perennial.
Euonymus fortunei	Wintercreeper		X		5		X	Hardy from zone 3 with protection. There are many varieties of this handsome species, including *minimus, coloratus* and *vegetus. Acutus* is a very good climber. Choose the form that best suits your needs. Likes sun, but will tolerate part shade. Some have showy fruits or variegated leaves. Perennial.
Hedera helix baltica	Baltic Ivy		X		(4, if protected, 5)	X	X	A hardier version of the usual English Ivy, with smaller leaves. Does not like sun, will do well even in deep shade. Protect from winter sun (spray with anti-dessicant to prevent loss of leaves during winter, but even if winterkilled, will grow back following spring). Can be used in sheltered and shady spot of terraces, but only as a ground cover. Perennial.
Iberis sempervirens	Candytuft		X		3		X	Pretty white flowers in low, compact clumps. Needs moisture. Keep dividing plants to have enough to cover whatever area you have. Slow grower so not for those who need quick cover for large areas. Perennial.
Ipomoea purpurea	Morning-glory		X		3		X	Beautiful and quick growing annual vine. Many varieties with varying colors and size. Heavenly Blue, Scarlett O'Hara and Pearly Gates are good. Flowers from early summer until frost. Needs full sun; needs support to climb. Perennial species cannot be grown in cool climates; have very large root systems.
Juniperus horizontalis	Creeping Juniper	X			2	X		Likes sun and sandy soil. Many good varieties: *douglasi, plumosa,* "Bar Harbor." Blue fruit. Showy ground cover. Perennial.
Lonicera japonica halliana	Hall's Japanese Honeysuckle	X			4		X	Sun or shade with slightly moist soil. A semi-evergreen. White, fragrant flowers in the summer. Needs plenty of room as it's a rampant grower! Other species that are suitable are *L. henryi* and *L. sempervirens.* Perennial.

Latin Name	Common Name		Zone				Description
Lysimachia nummularia	Moneywort, Creeping Charlie	X	4			X	Must have moist soil but will do well in part shade or full sun. It's a fast creeper with stems that root easily at the joints. A weed to many gardeners, but has much to say for it, for its ease of culture and yellow flowers in summer. Perennial.
Pachysandra terminalis	Japanese Spurge	X	5	X		X	Sun or shade, but does best in shade. White flowers in late spring. Handsome, shiny leaves; spreads rapidly. Great as a background for spring bulbs. Plant two or three clusters of daffodils in the Pachysandra for a delightful spring show. Perennial.
Parthenocissus tricuspidata	Boston Ivy	X	4	X		X	Far hardier than any of the English ivies. Tolerates sun, shade, any soil and city pollution. A quick and dense climber, with brilliantly colored leaves in the fall. Several varieties available. *P. quinquefolia*, known as "Virginia Creeper," is also a fast grower and with fabulous fall color. Neither species is a real ivy, but performs better under harsh conditions. Perennials.
Polygonum auberti	Silverlace Vine	X	4			X	Sun or part shade, with masses of fragrant, white flowers in summer. Needs support to climb and ruthless pruning to keep within bounds. Attracts bees. Perennial.
Quamoclit sloteri	Cardinal Climber	X	5	X		X	Free-blooming annual vine with red flowers. *Q. pennata*, Cypress Vine, another annual vine in the same family has a dantier growth habit.
Rosa wichuraiana	Memorial Rose	X	4	X		X	An old-timer! Trailing, prostrate, semi-evergreen rose with fragrant, white flowers in late summer. Needs room and sun. Perennial.
Sedum	Stonecrop, Liveforever	X	4			X	Many of the creeping sedum species make excellent ground covers for dry, sunny areas. They form low, dense mats where few other plants would survive, especially in rock gardens. *S. acre* will quickly take over; *S. spurium, S. sarmentosum, S. sieboldi* are among many good species. Flowers are a side bonus. Perennial.
Thunbergia alata	Black-eyed Susan	X	8		X		A perennial grown as an annual in cool climates (zones 4 to 7); can be used as a ground cover or a low vine as it does not grow very tall, but rather rambles along. Sun or part shade but moist soil.
Thymus serpyllum	Mother-of-Thyme	X	4	X		X	Many varieties of this fragrant plant which is great as a spreading mat or in-between stepping stones. Likes dry soil and sun, but tolerates shade well. Purple or red flowers in summer. Perennial.
Vinca minor	Running Myrtle or Periwinkle	X	5	X		X	Will stand sun better than Pachysandra, not to mention Ivy! Good for window boxes and hanging baskets. Pretty blue flowers in spring. *V. major*, however, can only be used as a ground cover in warm climates. Its variegated form is often used in containers and window boxes if treated as an annual in the north. Very effective when combined with flowers. Needs warmth and sun, so restrict this species to the terrace. Perennial.
Vitis	Grape	X	depends on variety			X	Sunny city backyards are filled with grape-covered arbors, but they do well on sunny terraces also. Good-looking foliage, and, after a few years, tasty fruit as well. Grow them against a fence or wall, training them on wires or using ready-made fasteners. Try them for fun. Many varieties. Choose the one best suited to your climate and location. Perennial.
Wisteria sinensis	Chinese Wisteria	X	4			X	As good as Silverlace Vine to hide any eyesore or cover a pergola, except that it's far trickier to get it to bloom. Handsome foliage. Give it support to climb the first couple of years. Perennial.

HOW TO PLANT SHRUBS AND TREES

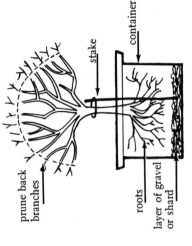

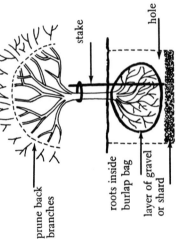

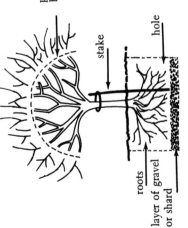

BARE ROOT

1. Soak roots in water.
2. Dig deep and wide hole.
3. Spread roots at 4- to 6-inch depth.
4. Prune back branches a good deal to make up for loss of roots.

BALLED AND BURLAPPED

1. Dig deep and wide hole to hold burlapped ball and still leave plenty of space around.
2. Cut rope and loosen burlap.
3. Plant leaving burlap on. (It will decompose shortly).
4. Prune back branches lightly.

CONTAINER GROWN

1. Dig hole large enough to fit root ball.
2. *Gently* remove root ball from container.
3. Prune back branches lightly.

OF IMPORTANCE FOR ALL TYPES OF PLANTING:

Stake tree if it is of good size or will be located in windy area. Wrap trunks of larger trees with burlap. Spread all roots carefully and cut off any broken ones. Always dig a hole bigger than the root ball, and spread a layer of gravel or broken clay bits at the bottom for good drainage. Cover with good soil about halfway to the top, then water thoroughly. Add remaining soil and tamp down. (This is to get rid of air pockets.) Do not add soil right up to the level of the ground. Leave a "saucer" depression around the tree to catch water. Mulch at least three inches. Water again and sprinkle top of tree as well. Plant trees and shrubs at same depth as in nursery. This can be spotted by the mark on the trunk or stem which denotes where the soil level was. Keep it at the same level. Don't overwater but check daily to see that soil doesn't get dry.

Of Concern to All
City Gardeners

25. PRUNING

To the new gardener, pruning is often a fearful, mysterious science, coped with by simply ignoring it. This shouldn't be, because pruning is based on common sense. It's not complicated, it's certainly not mysterious and it's easy to do. All that is required is knowledge of *why* pruning is necessary, *when* to do it and *how* to go about it.

There are two major reasons for pruning. The first is aesthetic. We prune for beauty: size, shape and maximum blooming. Shrubs become too tall or too wide for their location, or have straggly branches going off in different directions, or need to be rejuvenated by having some of their old wood cut down to the base. Flowering shrubs are kept healthy and blooming by careful pruning. Hedges need trimming to look neat and remain within the space allocated for them. In the country, plants can be left to grow on their own, reaching whatever size they choose—indeed, they look far handsomer that way in my personal opinion—but in the city, where every inch of space is precious, plant growth has to be controlled. Of course, the ideal is for the wise gardener to stick with plants he knows will not grow beyond a certain size, thereby eliminating pruning, but if he bought the wrong plants for his garden layout or if he inherited the previous owner's mistakes, he has to resort to pruning.

The second reason for pruning has to do with the health of the plants. Any dead, damaged or diseased branch must be cut off to ensure the continued vigor of the plant. This type of emergency pruning can be done any time of the year. If left unattended, pests and diseases find their way into the plant and can kill it. During the winter, you probably hardly set foot in the garden, but do force yourself to take a "walk" and inspect the shrubs periodically, especially after a storm or heavy rains. It takes only a few minutes for you to prune off a broken branch. In the case of tall trees in backyards, a professional tree service should be called in to saw off heavy limbs that have been damaged. Cabling, bracing or pruning of tall trees is not a job for amateurs. Special equipment is necessary, not to mention experience. If your backyard needs more sunlight and you wish to thin out a tree, this can be done, but it is also a job for the experts.

Proper tools are vital for easy pruning. All that the city gardener needs is a pruning saw for small tree limbs, a pruning lopper for all types of branches, a pair of hand pruning shears for small, twiggy branches and suckers, hedge shears (only if you have a hedge; otherwise this tool butchers plants) and a spray can of pruning paint to be applied to pruning cuts that are over one inch in diameter. This prevents disease from entering the tree via insects. A pole pruner with an extension rod is needed only if you have trees in your garden that are beyond your reach. I wouldn't bother buying one, however, since it's likely that such trees are of a size requiring professional handling.

Shrubs

While pruning dead, diseased or damaged limbs can and should be done any time during the year, most other pruning is done at specific times. Shrubs that bloom *after* June (called summer-flowering shrubs) are pruned when dormant, usually in early March, because these shrubs bloom on shoots of the current year's growth. In the case of shrubs that bloom *before* the end of June (called spring-flowering shrubs), pruning takes place immediately after blooming. Flowers on these shrubs bloom on shoots of the previous year or older. Behind all this is plain common sense. You don't want to prune a shrub at the wrong time of year because if you did, you wouldn't kill the plant but it just wouldn't flower. So before you start pruning any shrub, first remember *when* during the year it normally flowers, and you'll know the proper time to prune it.

Evergreens are in a category by themselves when it comes to pruning. They should be pruned only in case of disease or storm damage; they are best left alone otherwise. Since little can be done to contain their size without resorting to mutilation, it's important that the proper varieties be planted in the first place. This way you avoid having a magnificent evergreen take over a garden and darken the entire back of the house (or the front, as is so often seen in older parts of cities). Transplanting large, old evergreens is not only extremely costly but the chances of success are slim.

If you can't grow anything in your backyard because of such an oversized evergreen, have it cut down and donate it at Christmas to your community center or a hospital. The guilt for such a drastic act rests squarely on the shoulders of the original owner, who should have known that trees meant to grow as giants in forests have no place in the typical tiny city backyard. If you have to cut down a tree, however, ask the advice of a professional landscape designer. No tree is more beautiful than an evergreen, or makes a finer background for a shady, naturalistic woodland garden. But if there is such dense shade that nothing will grow, take out the tree and make sure you inquire about the growth habit of the next evergreen you buy and its ultimate height at maturity.

Young evergreens should be allowed to have only one strong, central leader (that's the center branch that towers above the others). If two develop, select the bigger, more vigorous one and remove the other. Broad-leafed evergreens (like holly, laurel, andromeda) can be pruned lightly in early spring to keep them within bounds and maintain a neat appearance.

Many flowering shrubs grow as clumps and soon become a tangled mess, with flowers that are scarcer and smaller each year. To keep them young and vigorous, thin them out. This is done by cutting old stems right at the base, back to the point where they grow out of the ground. If you cut back one-third of the clump each year for three years, you will have new, healthy growth. Repeat this three-year schedule periodically as it seems necessary.

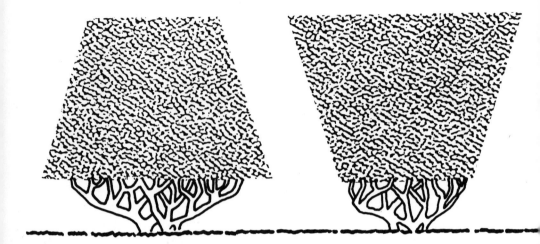
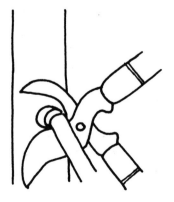
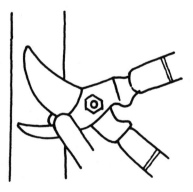

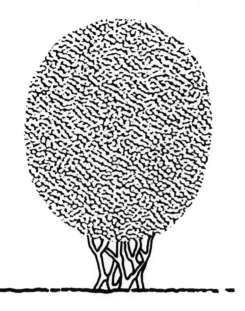

▲
Hedge pruning is a necessity for city gardeners with limited space. Too many hedges have a top-heavy, bare-bottom look, such as shown in the middle drawing, as a result of improper pruning. Extreme left illustrates correct pruning method, while sketch at extreme right is that of the shrub allowed to grow naturally, preferred by many gardeners who have plenty of space and little time to spare.

◀Branches of one to one-and-a-half inches in diameter can be easily removed with shears or lopper. The objective is a clean cut with the shortest stub possible, which demands proper use of the tool. Sketch at left shows improper method. The cutting blade is under the limb resulting in a ragged, larger stub. Sketch at right shows proper angle of tool. Cutting blade is on *top* and as close as possible to tree trunk. To get good leverage, insert limb as deeply into the blades as possible. Do *not* tear limb away or twist it free of trunk as this tears the bark, inviting pests and trouble.

Then there are shrubs that are lush and bushy on top but sadly naked down below. To rejuvenate these, especially if they have been neglected for many years, cut out a few branches at the base and trim the top unevenly so as to have as natural a look as possible. No crew cut, please! This method of thinning will make the plant bushier all over.

When pruning for shape, *go slowly*. Trim carefully and then stand back and take a good look. It's so easy to get carried away and cut more than is necessary. Then it takes a long time to undo the harm done. Know what your objective is when you're pruning. Pruning aimlessly is a waste of time and effort and is detrimental to the plant.

The following *spring-flowering* shrubs should be pruned immediately *after* blooming:

Azalea—Prune branches to get new growth. Remove suckers.

Barberry (*Berberis*)—Prune old wood.

Beautybush (*Kolkwitzia*)—Prune old wood.

Blueberry (*Vaccinium*)—Remove weak twigs.

Burningbush (*Euonymus*)—Remove crowded branches.

Deutzia—Follow three-year schedule (see page 105).

Enkianthus, Redvein (*Enkianthus campanulatus*)—Slight shaping at the most.

Firethorn (*Pyracantha*)—Prune only to control shape and size if you don't want to lose any of those beautiful berries.

Forsythia—Follow three-year schedule (see page 105).

Honeysuckle (*Lonicera fragrantissima*)—Follow the three-year schedule as often as needed to control rampant growth (see page 105).

Hydrangea (*H. macrophylla*)—If no spring flowers due to winter damage, wait until summer to prune. Never prune in winter or early spring. Cut old, woody plants to the ground.

Lilac (*Syringa*)—Follow the three-year schedule (see page 105). Remove all suckers.

Magnolia—Only prune occasionally to shape.

Rockspray (*Cotoneaster*)—Only prune to shape.

Snowbell (*Styrax*)—Prune to shape.

Spirea (*Spiraea*)—Follow three-year schedule (see page 105).

Viburnum—Prune to shape.

Weigela—Thin out new growth and prune old branches to prevent crowding.

Witch hazel (*Hamamelis mollis*)—Prune old wood.

The following *summer-flowering* shrubs should be pruned when dormant, in very *early spring:*

Abelia—Cut out crowded branches and wild shoots.

Beautyberry (*Callicarpa japonica*)—Prune stems about twelve inches from the ground each year.

Butterflybush (*Buddleia davidi*)—Cut stems to the ground each year.

Elaeagnus—Prune to shape every few years or so.

Heather (*Calluna*)—Cut stems down to the ground in very early spring.

Hibiscus—To obtain flowers, prune stems, leaving two buds.

Honeysuckle bush (*Diervilla*)—Prune to the ground to keep under control.

Hydrangea (*H. paniculata* var. *grandiflora*)—Prune back this summer-flowering species to a few buds if you need to thin out extra stems.

St. Johnswort (*Hypericum*)—Cut down crowded branches. Prune branches back, leaving two buds on each branch. This encourages new growth.

Spirea (*Spiraea*)—For summer-flowering varieties, cut back to a few buds and remove crowded stems.

Summersweet (*Clethra*)—Prune to shape.

Prune these *broad-leafed evergreens* in early spring:

Andromeda (*Pieris japonica*)—Prune lightly to promote new growth and to keep proper shape.

Box (*Buxus*)—Trim branches and stems to keep shrub bushy.

Camellia (*C. japonica* and *C. sasanqua*)—To get more flowers, cut out the old wood.

Holly—Go easy; trim only to control shape and size.

Holly osmanthus (*Osmanthus*)—Prune only to keep shape.

Leucothoe (*Leucothoë catesbaei*)—Cut old stems down when they get crowded.

Mountain laurel (*Kalmia*)—Cut old stems down to the ground periodically to encourage new growth.

Oleander (*Nerium oleander*)—Prune only to control size.

Privet (*Ligustrum*, evergreen and semi-evergreen varieties)—Prune to control size and shape. Cut four-year wood to the ground to promote new growth.

Rhododendron—Prune after flowering to encourage new growth and remove leggy stems in early spring.

Coniferous Evergreens

The less you touch these fine specimens, the better. If you must do any pruning, do it in the spring when new buds and shoots are formed. Don't touch the top leader (central branch) if you want the plant to get taller, but if you want a shorter, denser plant, cut the other candles (shoots that stick out) by half. Leave needles alone on pine trees; trim only the candles.

Fir (*Abies*)—Prune candles halfway to encourage side growth.

Hemlock (*Tsuga*)—Prune only if used as hedge.

Juniper (*Juniperus*)—Prune only to control shape and size.

Pine (*Pinus*)—Prune candles back halfway if new side growth is desired; leave alone otherwise.

Red Cedar (*Juniperus*)—Prune ragged branches in early spring and prune again in June to control size as needed.

Spruce (*Picea*)—Prune candles back halfway to encourage side growth.

Yew (*Taxus*)—Prune ragged branches in early spring; prune again only to control size and shape.

Reminder: Prune dead, damaged or diseased branches at *any* time during the year—the sooner after the damage is noticed, the better.

Trees

Trees on terraces and almost all trees in backyards can be pruned easily by the city gardener. Exceptions are the old, mature trees in backyards, which require professional care. If a tree is pruned when young and is encouraged to grow in a neat and airy shape, it will be strong and healthy and require virtually no care thereafter, other than the usual sucker growth (small twigs that grow from branches, on the trunk or at the base of trees). Just snip those away as they appear.

Where branches crisscross one another, remove the smaller, weaker one. Trees should be allowed only a few strong main branches, not only because this makes for a graceful shape, but also because the wind will be able to blow through the tree without causing damage to limbs. The strength of the tree will be concentrated only in its main branches. Pruning is just plain common sense, as mentioned earlier; there must always be a good reason for doing it. Once suckers are allowed to grow into branches, it becomes major surgery to cut them off. Twin leaders should also be corrected when young. The crotch formed by the two central branches invites splitting of the tree later on. Remove the weaker branch at the base of the crotch, letting the other central branch dominate the tree.

If a branch of a small tree or one shrub grows much faster than the others (there are always eager beavers in the plant world), cut it back to match the others. When pruning smaller branches, cut back to a main branch to avoid ugly stubs. When cutting off an entire limb, make the cut flush with the trunk, leaving as small a stub as possible without stripping the bark of the trunk. Spray with tree paint any cut over one inch in diameter. When trimming just a few inches off a branch, cut back to a cluster of leaves to make the cut almost invisible.

Train small, ornamental trees when young, for then is the time to start them off to an attractive shape. Remove all suckers and crisscrossing branches, leaving a few good "frame" branches that will determine the mature shape of the tree. Cut back a bit the remaining side branches, as well as the leader, in order to promote vigorous root growth.

26. SELECTION AND CARE OF TOOLS

One way to tell an experienced, knowledgeable gardener is by his tools. He has few of them and they're in tip-top condition. The amateur buys every new gadget in sight, paying no attention to quality or maintenance. If all these tools produced better results, there would be some point in adding yearly to the collection, but, sadly enough, the contrary is true.

Select tools with specific jobs in mind. Buy the best quality you can afford; with proper care, good tools last many years and do a better job. Wrap some bright-colored adhesive tape around the handles so that you won't forget to pick them up after the job is done. Keep tools clean by wiping them with an oily cloth, or fill a plastic container with one foot of sand saturated with crankcase oil; push the tools into the sand a few times. They'll be cleaned by the abrasive action of the sand and oiled at the same time to prevent rusting. Keep a lid on the container when not in use, or keep it in a sheltered place.

Here are the basic tools you'll need:

1. A trowel to dig small holes for flowers and vegetables.
2. A spade (squared-sided) or shovel (pointed-nosed) for digging larger holes for shrubs, small trees, large clumps of perennials.
3. A spading fork—a must for transplanting plants since it doesn't cut roots, as a shovel would.
4. A hoe to cultivate the soil in flower beds; it's also useful for breaking up small clumps of soil when winter is over. Use the back of the blade for this.
5. A cultivator with three or four prongs—great for loosening up the soil and for incorporating dry fertilizer into it. It comes with a long handle or hand-sized.
6. A pruning saw; the curved style for smaller limbs is sufficient.
7. A pruning lopper—these long-handled shears cut branches that don't require a saw, which covers 90 percent of your pruning.
8. A hand pruner, no bigger than a pair of scissors and as easy to use. It cuts small branches, twigs, perennials, etc.
9. Hedge shears—needed only if you have a hedge, as they should *never* be used to prune shrubs. The new cordless power-operated type is great.
10. A hose—indispensable for watering anywhere. Buy the most flexible kind, the easiest to handle in small spaces.

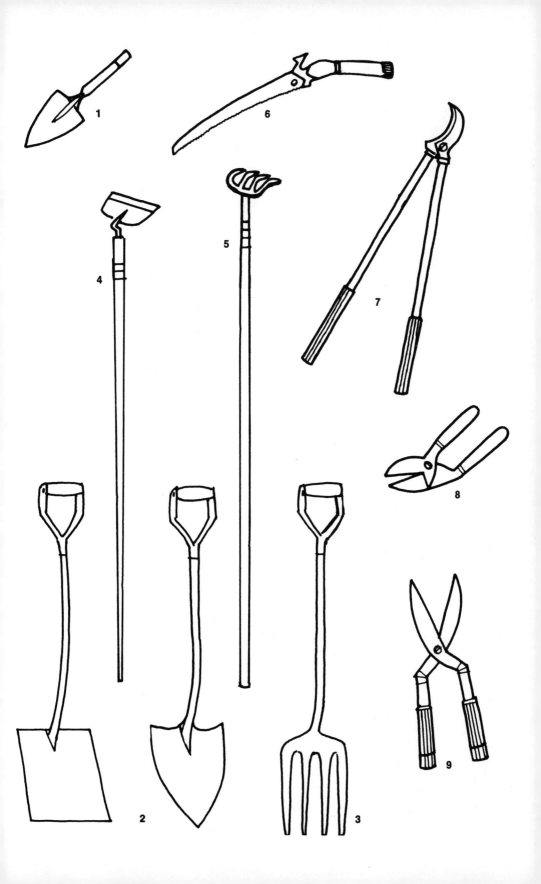

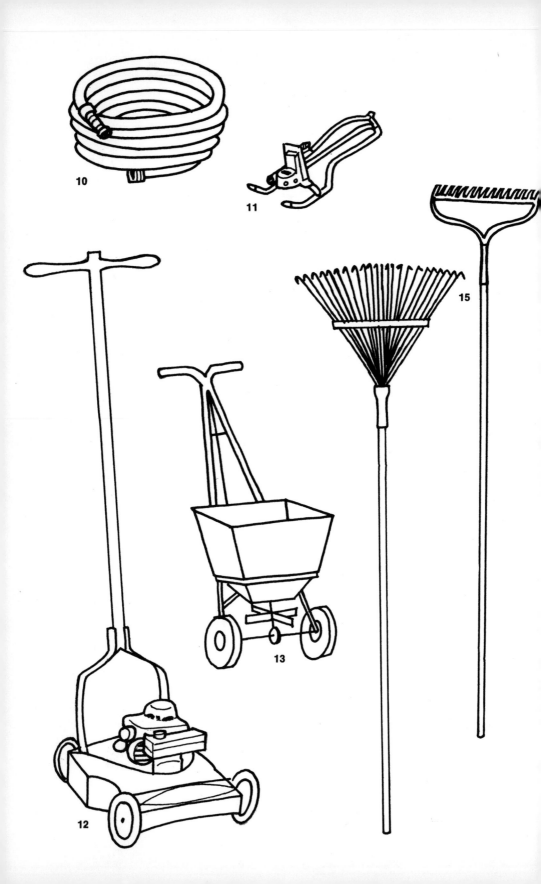

10

11

12

13

15

Get a good nozzle head that lets you control the type flow you need. Keep the hose coiled in an attractive wood tub near the outside water faucet, or suspend it from a special holder on the wall.

11. A sprinkler—if your garden is large enough to warrant one. It will do the watering job for you and is a necessity if you insist on keeping your lawn green during the summer.
12. A lawn mower—obviously needed only if you have a lawn.
13. A fertilizer spreader—needed only if you have a lawn.
14. Plastic pails—the two-gallon size, marked accordingly so you can measure fertilizer correctly. These pails do all sorts of jobs around the small garden. They replace a wheelbarrow for carrying debris, leaves, faded flowers, tools, small plants, soil and other material. If yours is an extra-large backyard garden or terrace, you might consider one of those small carts with large rubber wheels.
15. Rakes: the steel rake is used to smooth the surface of the soil to a fine texture, while the lawn rake is for raking leaves. Both types come in several sizes. The smallest-sized steel rake could replace a cultivator, and there's no need to buy both.

This basic list covers all a gardener really needs to do a good job. Buy only those tools that you will need. If yours is a small balcony with only container plants, obviously you will require very little: a trowel, a hand cultivator, a hand pruner and a hose will see you through nicely.

It doesn't matter where you store your tools, so long as they are kept dry. A toolshed is great if you have the place for it; otherwise, a watertight container with a lid will do. If you want to hide the container, keep it inside a wicker hamper.

I did not include a sprayer for insecticides because I don't believe that spraying should be encouraged. For a large garden, where spraying is an absolute must, buy the smallest sprayer available and the easiest type to use. It will prevent you from mixing too large a quantity of chemicals, which makes disposal of excess difficult. And if it's easy to use, you'll avoid accidents. Ask your garden center supplier for the safest model. For small jobs, aerosol spray cans are available.

Power tools are great for jobs in the country. The city gardener has no use for them, however. On the rare occasion when he might need one, he can easily rent it for a small hourly rate. An exception is a lawn mower—which you use weekly if you have a lawn—or a hedge trimmer if you have a long hedge to keep neat. But whether you own or rent, keep all power tools out of reach of children and pets. Be careful yourself when using them. They're not toys. Read the manufacturer's directions carefully.

27. HOW TO POT PLANTS

To some, it may seem incredible that not everybody knows how to pot a plant; but then again, why should they? Expertise in any field comes with practice. A task becomes a breeze after a while, but let's remember that we *all* had to learn at one time—the greatest experts included. Container gardening forms the backbone of city gardens; indeed, on terraces it's often the entire garden. Correct potting is essential to the health of plants, and it's easy if you follow a few simple procedures.

Should you have to do the potting in full sunlight, turn your back to the sun in such a way that the plant is shielded from the direct rays while you're working. Sun and wind dry roots quickly, which aggravates transplant shock. If possible, it's best to wait until your garden is in the shade before you do any planting. Have everything ready: pots (absolutely clean; new clay ones should be soaked in water for a few hours before use, since they are porous and would draw moisture immediately from the newly potted plant); soil; plants (wait until the last minute to remove them from old pots); trowel (to help ease the plant out of its old pot and to pour soil into the new container; in the case of large tubs, use a shovel to save time); shards (broken bits of old clay pots that have been rinsed in a solution of water and household bleach, or use gravel instead); coarsely shredded sphagnum moss. Protect the terrace floor with newspapers or a plastic sheet.

Now let's suppose you've just bought three geraniums and three pots of ivy—all in small pots—and you'd like to combine them in a large container to make a good-looking "statement" in a sunny corner of the garden. Here's the procedure to follow:

1. Cover the drainage hole and the rest of the bottom of the container with a layer of shards or gravel. The thickness of the layer depends on the size of the container. A single layer is enough for pots up to five inches; add another layer for larger ones. Tubs and barrels require four to six inches of drainage material. (*Note:* the size of a pot is based on its diameter at the top, measured on the *inside* of the rim. The height of the pot has nothing to do with it, as this can vary quite a bit while still retaining the same diameter on top.)

2. In the case of very large pots (anything over ten inches), cover the broken bits of clay with a layer of coarse sphagnum moss to prevent the soil from sifting through the shards and out the drainage hole.

3. Now fill one-third to one-half of the pot with soil. Exactly how much to put in at this point depends on how large the root balls of the plants are.

4. Remove plants from their old pots, since they are now ready to be put into their new containers. The easiest way of getting a plant out of its original pot is to turn it upside down, firmly holding the stem of the plant between your fingers the whole time, and to tap the rim of the pot gently until the plant falls out on its own. *Don't* try to help matters by pulling on the stem. If the plant is so pot-bound that nothing budges it, break the pot and ease the plant out.

5. When combining several plants, as in this case, arrange them first in the pot to see if they will fit. Each root ball should have room to grow. Space the three ivy plants near the edge of the container, equally apart, and then put the three geraniums together in the center. If all the plants fit, keep adding more soil, firming it around each plant as you do so.

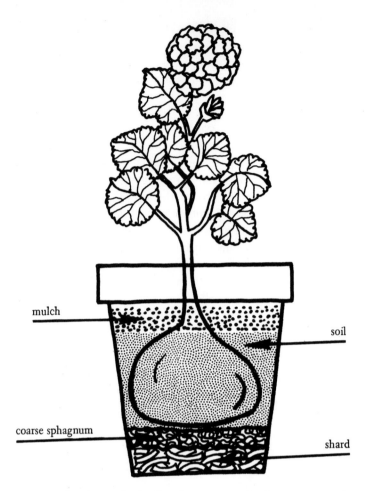

mulch

soil

coarse sphagnum

shard

Potting plants properly the first time, or repotting later on, goes a long way towards insuring healthy growth. Shard or gravel provides drainage, coarse sphagnum prevents soil from washing out of the pot, and mulch on the surface keeps the soil and roots cool and moist during the summer and prevents heaving from frost in winter. Leave space between mulch and the rim of the pot to facilitate thorough watering.

6. Don't fill the pot with soil right up to the very top of the rim. Leave about half an inch (several inches in the case of tubs), so that the water won't run off when you're watering the plant. Also, if you're going to add a layer of mulch on the surface (an excellent idea for all medium to large containers), allow for this when adding the soil.

7. Tap the bottom of the pot gently to help settle the soil. Water thoroughly until it comes out the drainage hole. Tap the pot again to eliminate any possible air holes, and that's it—you're finished.

After you have potted a few plants, you will be able to follow this procedure without even thinking about each step. Having a place to work with all the necessary ingredients at hand makes potting a quick job. Annuals that have small roots can be crowded together without suffering, but perennials should be given plenty of room, as should shrubs and small trees.

Save old or cracked clay pots to use as drainage material. This way you won't have to buy gravel. The rule of thumb for a pot-bound plant is to put it in a pot one size larger than the one it was in before. On the other hand, if you see that there is still plenty of soil around the root ball, leave it in the same size container.

It's well worth the effort, for the results that you get, to re-pot all the plants you buy. Those that go directly into the ground have no problems, but those that will be grown in containers are best given a fresh start. Very few plants sold today are properly potted in a top-quality soil mixture. Nurseries are in the business of growing plants and selling them. It's up to the consumer to pick up from there. I have bought plants from "discount" places and from fancy boutiques. It made no difference. I seldom found any drainage material at the bottom of the pot—sometimes only one small bit of clay barely covering the hole—and the soil mixtures were poor. Many plants were so root-bound that inches of the roots hung outside the bottom hole. The experienced gardener takes all this in stride, even expects it, and goes about repotting the plant properly. The innocent beginner, understandably, does nothing and wonders why his plants are not thriving.

Here are a few suggestions to find out if a plant is properly potted: When you water the plant, does water go clear through the pot in a flash? Inferior mixture. Repot the plant in fresh soil.

Or does the water do the opposite, just sitting on the surface without going down? Again, repot the plant in fresh soil.

Remove the plant from its pot; is it all roots, tightly coiled, with little or no soil? Or are roots sticking out the bottom hole?

That's a pot-bound plant if ever you'll see one. Repot in a one-size-larger container.

If, when you remove the plant from the pot, you don't see a layer of drainage material, add one before putting the plant back.

Correct potting of a plant is a little like feeding a computer. The results you get are based on what you put into it.

All containers, small or large, should have drainage holes, but if for some reason you put a plant in an ornamental watertight pot, double the thickness of the layer of drainage material. Water it very sparingly. You'll have to guess when the water has reached the bottom of the roots—a situation that doesn't make for good gardening (unless the container is transparent). Cacti and succulents are the best plants to choose for such containers, as they require very little water; therefore, you can err on the side of underwatering. Or go clear to the other extreme and plant varieties that thrive in swamps and bogs and like to have their "feet" wet. But I would heartily recommend staying away from such containers in the first place. Instead, try double-potting.

Double-potting is nothing more than inserting one pot inside another. The inside pot holds the plant and is made of plain clay or plastic. It has drainage holes. The outer pot is the fancy, decorative, watertight kind that can add a great deal of charm and beauty to a terrace. The trick is to hide the inner pot, making it look as though the plant were growing directly out of the larger container. This is easily done. First spread a layer of gravel at the bottom of the larger container (to catch the drainage water from the inside pot). Slip the plain pot inside the container, resting it on the gravel, and fill in the empty spaces between the two pots with a mulch of some sort. This can be decorative gravel, shredded bark or coarse sphagnum moss. Continue the mulch right up to the top of the containers. Cover the surface of the soil with a layer of the same mulch or green sheet moss. Double-potting is not only attractive, but the plant is kept cool during the hot summer months, and moisture remains in the soil much longer.

A word of caution about double-potting: it's best limited to pots of small to medium size. These can easily be emptied of excess water in the event of a heavy rainfall. The drainage layer inside the larger container is adequate to handle the normal overflow of water from the smaller pot inside, but not from a long

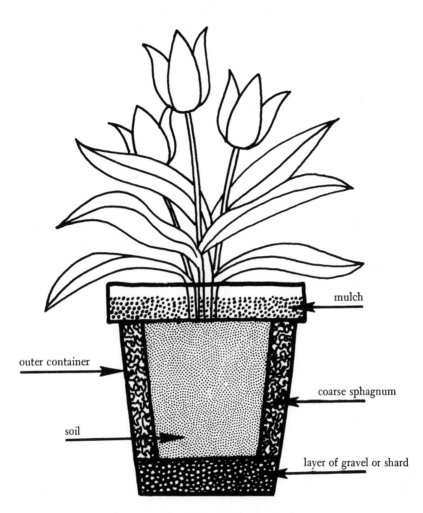

mulch

outer container

coarse sphagnum

soil

layer of gravel or shard

Double potting is the city gardener's best friend for both esthetic and horti-cultural reasons. Putting a plain clay or plastic pot (with drainage holes) inside an ornamental container, not only improves the appearance of a ter-race or backyard, but prevents soil from drying out quickly. A thick layer of gravel at the bottom of the outer container absorbs drainage water from the inner pot, contributing needed humidity to the plant while preventing its roots from rotting.

drenching rain. Water under these circumstances can accumulate inside the container and drown the plant. If you're alert to this danger, you can rush to the rescue of the plant by tipping the container slightly and letting excess water run out. One can see why large ceramic tubs would be impossible to handle in this manner.

Root Pruning

There comes a time when you can repot no further. Your pet plant which started as a tiny seedling has proven its robust health by growing and growing. You showed your appreciation by repotting it every few years into larger containers, but now the point of no return has been reached. You want to keep it in its present container, but it's pot-bound once again. The answer is to root-prune it. It sounds drastic and it is, because it's major surgery for the plant, but you'd be surprised at how well most plants take it. Here's all you do:

1. Remove the plant from its pot. (This is easier said than done when the plant is old and *really* pot-bound! It took two men to help pull out an old gardenia plant of mine, which I root-pruned drastically; it's now thriving.)

2. With a sharp knife, cut off a layer of roots from the bottom and the sides. Be certain you cut off enough roots so that when the plant is put back in its pot there will be plenty of space for future new roots to spread out. If you cut off too little, you'll only have to do this procedure over again in a year.

3. If you're dealing with a large plant in a tub, as I was with my gardenia, you'll have to use a saw to cut the roots, as they will be far too tough for a knife to handle. A small saw does the job quickly and efficiently. Lacking a saw, a large carving knife with a serrated edge will also do the job.

4. Repot the plant in fresh soil. Now is as good a time as any to do this, since you've got the plant out of its pot anyway.

5. Water the plant thoroughly. Wait a month or longer before giving it any fertilizer. After all, it's just gone through quite a shock and needs time to get over it—but it will. I reduced the root ball of my gardenia by at least

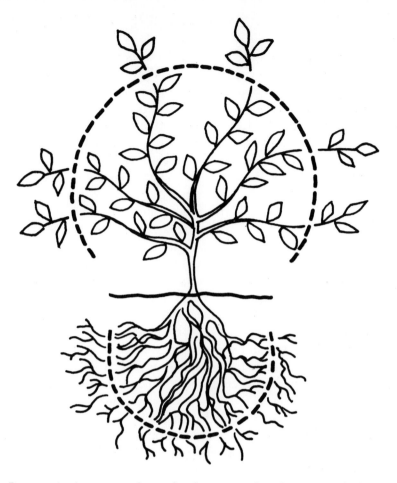

Root pruning is necessary when a plant becomes pot-bound and can no longer be repotted into a larger container. It simply involves cutting off from one quarter to one third of the roots on the sides and bottom, and the same amount from the top growth.

a third all-around, and, as mentioned, it's in vigorous health and blooming.

6. To compensate for the loss of roots and to help in its recovery, trim back the top of the plant. Cutting back part of the branches also gives you an opportunity to shape the plant and give it a neater appearance.

Potting mixtures for plants in containers appear to be as varied as recipes for stew, but a good, all-around mixture is: two parts loam, one part peat moss and one part sand (perlite is an excellent substitute for sand and far lighter in weight, highly recommended for terraces). Add a handful each of limestone and bone meal and you've got it. To be technical and for larger quantities, it's a five-inch potful of bone meal and a four-inch potful of limestone for each bushel of soil mixture. Mix all the ingredients thoroughly before using.

This mixture is good for most plants. However, for those that are acid-loving, like most evergreens, begonias, and so forth, mix one part loam, one part peat moss and one part sand (or perlite). Add the bone meal but skip the limestone. If you grow cacti or succulents, mix one part loam, one part sand (or perlite) and a half-part small pieces of broken clay, plus the bone meal and limestone. A richer formula for containers located on exceptionally windy and sunny high-rise terraces is given on pages 81–82. Excess wind and sun dry out the soil very quickly, and a somewhat richer mixture is sometimes advisable.

Perhaps you're wondering about some of the terms used for the mixtures. Loam is soil, very broadly speaking. You buy it as "potting soil" in large plastic bags, already sterilized so that you needn't worry about weeds and bugs and such. It should not be used all by itself, which is why you need the other ingredients mentioned. By sand is meant builder's sand, so don't go to the nearest beach for your supply. Better still, buy perlite and use that instead. Vermiculite is also a good substitute for sand but I prefer perlite, or a mixture of half vermiculite and half perlite. Sand is so heavy to carry and to handle that I strongly discourage any city dweller from using it, but I mention it in case substitutes may not be available in your locality.

Buy finely shredded peat moss, not the coarse grade. The coarse variety is good to use as filler between pots when you're double-potting, for when kept moist it's additional protection in keeping plants watered during vacations or in hot weather. But use only the fine grade in a soil mixture.

Bone meal is a safe, slow-acting fertilizer that is a permanent enrichment to the soil. It's rich in nitrogen and phosphoric acid and is good for all plants. Limestone is a soil conditioner that counteracts acidity (which is why it's omitted for acid-loving plants) by keeping the soil "sweet," and it also helps in the decomposition of organic matter.

Both limestone and bone meal are available in garden supply centers. Buy small quantities, as a little goes a long way with each of them.

28. HOW AND WHEN TO WATER

Although watering is covered many times in this book, it bears repeating under its own heading. As with all other phases of gardening, there is no mystique about it. Watering is based on common sense. You water a plant when it needs it, the same way you get a drink of water when you feel thirsty. You don't drink water at the same time every day; similarly, you don't water plants on a robot-like basis. Each form of gardening, backyard, terrace and container, requires a different approach determined by such factors as rain, wind and sun, not to mention the types of plants—so let's take one at a time.

The backyard garden is generally shady and sheltered from high winds because of surrounding tall buildings. Flower beds are bottomless, unlike those on a terrace, and therefore the soil doesn't dry out quickly. Spring rains take care of the moisture required by plants as they begin their new growth. If there is little or no rain, you have to water. Your eyes and your fingers will tell you if the soil in your garden is dry. Dig a few inches, pick up a handful of soil and see how it looks in your hand. If it's fine and powdery and slips right through your fingers like sand, the soil needs watering, but it's more likely that in early spring it will form a ball of mud and will not need any additional moisture.

Permanent plantings (trees, shrubs, perennials) sink their roots deeply into the soil, drawing moisture from way below the surface. Not so annuals, which are shallow-rooted. When you first plant annuals in late spring/early summer, water thoroughly at planting time and regularly thereafter until the cooler and shorter days of fall begin. You might well ask what is meant by "regularly." There can be no foolproof answer. Too much depends on the amount of rain during the week, the intensity of the sun or the lack of it and the condition of your soil. The best and only sure way to tell is simply by sticking your fingers in the soil and determining for yourself. If the soil feels moist, leave it alone; if it's dry, water it. Hot, dry spells during the summer may make it necessary for you to water several times a week. Obviously, soil in exposed, sunny areas will dry out much faster than that under shady trees. Again, common sense prevails.

When you do water, water deeply. A mere sprinkling of the soil is a waste of time and does no good at all; indeed, it forces the plant roots to grow near the surface of the soil in their search for moisture instead of growing deeply into the ground as they should. Let water from the hose trickle slowly for an hour around trees, permanent shrubs and perennials; half an hour will do for annuals. A soaker-hose is a good investment, and it is inexpensive if you have several large flower beds. It's made of canvas, through which a gentle, slow, controlled flow of water seeps. Coil it around the base of plants or down the center of flower beds. One of its advantages is that the water flows evenly through the fabric, the *entire* length of the hose, as opposed to just the open end of a regular hose. This makes it possible to water a large area without moving the hose. A perforated plastic hose is based on the same principle but is not as flexible and easy to handle as the canvas kind.

The terrace garden depends on water for its very life, and that means you. Even when it rains, the water quickly evaporates because the soil is not deep, as it is in a backyard. And rainfall can be deceiving. Try putting an empty coffee can in the middle of the terrace next time it rains, and then measure how much fell. You'll be surprised at how little it is. It takes quite a shower to accumulate one inch of rain.

Sun and wind gang up on terrace plants to deprive them of valuable moisture. They become dehydrated quickly unless you replace that lost moisture. Also, pollution accumulation has to be washed off. In short, have a hose that's in good working condition, because you'll be using it a lot!

In early spring or later, depending on your locality, after you've cleaned up the terrace of winter debris (see chapter 24), give all the plants a thorough root watering and shower the foliage. Thereafter, let the weather be your guide. As summer approaches, the soil in the flower beds will start to dry out much faster, and watering will become a daily chore. Severe heat spells may necessitate twice-a-day watering. But again, let your fingers be the final authority. When scratching into the soil, you will quickly know if watering is needed.

Try not to wait until the signs of dryness become too obvious. Drooping leaves, cracks in the soil, soil shrunken away from the sides of containers—all these indicate that it's way past time for a good soaking. Plants may not necessarily die, but it imposes the kinds of stress on them that most certainly will rob them of vigor and good health. Make an inspection tour of your plants at least once a day and play safe. Water the beds deeply so that the roots get moisture all the way down to the bottom. Finish off by sprinkling the foliage of all trees and shrubs and hose the terrace flooring. This increases the humidity in the immediate area of the plants.

Container plants are found everywhere in city gardens, especially on terraces that have no room for built-in flower beds. Small trees and shrubs are grown in tubs and barrels, flowers in wooden boxes or large pots. Whatever the container, it's exposed to the elements from all sides and the amount of soil in it is strictly limited, all of which adds up to quick dehydration.

The smaller the container, the more often it needs watering. A small clay pot may need watering twice a day, a large barrel only once a week—but again, back to the finger test. Let it determine for you how dry or wet the soil is. If you've had a light shower and the surface of the soil feels wet, don't take it for granted that it's equally moist several inches down. Dig up a small wedge to see for yourself. Use a tablespoon for large tubs. Remember, the roots are down *below* and a sprinkling of water on top doesn't do them any good.

Keep watering a container until you see water coming out the drainage hole. This way you'll know you've thoroughly moistened the entire root system. Wait until the top few inches feel dry again before repeating the operation. Plastic pots, being nonporous, retain moisture far longer than do those made of unglazed clay, so act accordingly. If you don't care for the looks of plastic, insert a plastic pot inside a clay one. Ornamental metal containers are heat traps, so stay away from them. Save those antique metal urns for indoor plants.

Mulching is your best friend. Spread it on the surface of all your medium to large containers. This goes for window boxes and hanging baskets as well. A mulch not only prevents weeds, but holds in the precious moisture *and* keeps the soil cool. Choose an attractive mulch such as pine bark (nuggets for tubs and the finely shredded type for small containers), buckwheat hulls or green sheet moss.

29. HOW MUCH TIME IS ALL THIS GARDENING GOING TO TAKE?

You would think that the size of your backyard garden or your terrace would determine how much time you have to devote to its maintenance, but this is by no means true. You can have a large garden planted with a variety of shrubs and ground covers and a few containers of annuals, together with a good deal of outdoor furniture to create a handsome terrace, which will demand fewer hours of care than a smaller garden with many flower beds and clipped hedges.

Expect to spend more time working in your garden during early spring—or whenever all danger of frost is over—than any other time of year, because this is the main planting time for city dwellers. The garden is cleaned up, replacements are made as needed and annuals go into the ground or containers to "do their thing" until late fall. Maintenance now takes over, and how much of it you'll have during the summer months depends on several factors.

Watering. You'll spend much more time at it on a terrace than in a backyard, for reasons already explained in other chapters. If the summer is a hot one, and yours is a southern or western exposure, plan on daily watering of all plants. The more plants you have, the longer watering will take you, but count on about half an hour for a small terrace—less for a balcony, more for a large terrace or penthouse. The shady backyard garden can get by on deep once-a-week watering for beds, more often for containers. If it rains, you get a break, but it had better be a good, heavy shower, or it's of little good. Don't guess. Use the coffee-can checkup method described on page 126.

Plant material. The *kinds* of plants you have are an important factor in maintenance. Anything that requires frequent pruning or clipping is time-consuming. If the right species and varieties of trees and shrubs are selected for their site, practically no maintenance is needed other than watering. Ground covers, once established, are totally self-sufficient. Vines, again depending on which kind, can be anywhere from no work to constant pruning. Flowers are most demanding. Perennials have to be dug up and divided for maximum blooms, sometimes every year, but at least every three years. Annuals need to be watered frequently because of their shallow root systems, and if you want a colorful show all summer long, faded flowers should be picked off.

"Housekeeping." This covers all those little nitty-gritty jobs that gardeners never talk about because it's plain boring, but necessary nevertheless. The paved area of your garden has to be swept and/or hosed down to wash away the dirt, soot and whatever else falls from city skies (or the upstairs neighbors). Even with heavy mulching, expect a few weeds to pop up. Beds should be kept neat and clean, not only for aesthetic reasons, but also for control of pests and diseases. This pest control will take up less of your time if you practice preventive medicine by keeping a sharp eye out for signs of any mischief. Give shrubs a good hosing down periodically to discourage pests from settling in your garden.

If you want to keep your garden in tip-top condition, I would certainly advise you to figure on a minimum of three hours a week for maintenance, most of which will go for watering. If your terrace or backyard is large, the sky is the limit. It all depends on you, on how much time you can afford to spend and *wish* to spend.

I strongly suggest that unless gardening as such is your hobby, you start modestly and work your way up as you find out for yourself how much time it all takes. We all work at different paces and in varying ways and methods. Stop adding to your garden (presuming you have the space) when you feel it becomes a burden rather than a pleasure to care for it.

Those interested in the absolute minimum maintenance imaginable should rely on trees, shrubs, ground covers and slow-growing vines for instant greenery and coverage. If color is desired, a few spring bulbs that keep coming back each year and several containers of annuals will complete the look you want. If careful thought is given to the selection and groupings of these undemanding plants, you will be amazed at the handsome results you can obtain.

30. THE COMPOST PILE

If you live in the country, making your own compost pile is simple. You choose an out-of-sight spot in the garden and use it as your private dumping ground for raked leaves, dead plants, grass clippings, weeds you've pulled out, leftovers from pruning, etc. Some people also add so-called "clean garbage" from the kitchen—anything that would be thrown into the garbage except cans, bottles, fats and meat scraps—but I personally don't recommend this because it invites rodents and unpleasant odors unless one is careful to bury this refuse deep in the pile each time one deposits it.

The easiest and laziest way to make a compost pile is to keep adding to it and then leave it alone for a year, after which it will have turned into dark, rich, decomposed leaf mold, the best soil conditioner. A quicker way is to alternate layers of dumped leaves and such with a layer of soil, a sprinkling of limestone and a commercially available "activator," which claims to speed decomposition of the material. Turning the heap over several times a year also speeds the process, as does making a hole right through the center of the pile by sticking a pole into it and pulling it out. This is to allow water to seep into the pile, keeping it moist. For the same reason, don't give the pile a smooth, flat top; it should be concave in the center, so that rainwater is trapped there and slowly seeps down. I've never bothered with this complicated layering technique because, in all honesty, I don't have the time and energy. These I save for the more essential gardening chores I have to do.

I do keep two compost piles going at the same time, however, in order to have one in the process of "cooking" while the other is available for immediate use. You know it's ready when you can no longer recognize leaves as leaves, twigs as twigs, etc. It needn't be in a fine, pulverized state, but it should be broken down enough to be easily incorporated into the soil, where it will further decompose.

Now all of this is fine in the country, but what about the city? Who's got the room to build a compost heap, let alone two? Obviously, anything on a large scale is out of the question—but on the other hand, not as much leaf mold is needed, so it's all in proportion. What can be done is to use two large plastic garbage cans (two small ones will do if space is really limited) as containers for compost piles. Since good drainage is important, drill holes at the bottom of the cans, Swiss-cheese fashion. Don't keep lids on, as the compost must be kept moist (although it's O.K. to cover them at night if you're concerned about animals and such in backyards).

If yours is a backyard garden, you'll have leaves to put into the containers, as well as weeds, clippings, dead annuals, tops of bulbs (after they've yellowed and fallen off) and vegetable scraps, such as the outer leaves of lettuce one always discards, tops of carrots, pea pods, potato peelings and so forth. Stick to this kind of "clean" organic garbage; do not use the compost container as a regular garbage can. If you do, it won't do the compost any good and your standing with the neighbors will not be at an all-time high when the breeze blows their way—not to mention the trouble you'll have with insects and pests.

Since the compost piles are so small, you can do the layering bit. Start the piles with a couple of inches of soil at the bottom, alternating soil and compost material until you reach the top. Make it a ratio of about three to one: three inches of compost material to one inch of soil. It's also a good idea to sprinkle on some all-around fertilizer and a bit of limestone each time you add the soil. You will then have a good, rich leaf mold mixture in a hurry. What some people forget is that a compost pile is only as beneficial as the ingredients that go into it. In six months you should be able to use these two compost piles to enrich the soil in your garden. Afterward, get on the schedule of letting one pile "cook" while the other is being used.

Spread the compost everywhere you have plants and scratch

it well into the soil. Your plants will get a new lease on life. When you water the garden, turn the hose on the piles to keep them evenly moist, and use a long-handled cultivator to turn the mixtures over a few times during the year. If there is no way to hide the plastic cans—and their looks admittedly add little to the garden—use bottomless redwood boxes instead, set directly on the soil, or specially treated boxes with drainage holes.

It makes little sense to have a compost pile on a tiny terrace or balcony. It would take up space that could be used by ornamental plants, and anyway, where would you use the compost material when it's ready? So little soil conditioner is needed each year that a small bag of leaf mold purchased locally is sufficient to enrich the few containers in these small gardens.

Where larger terraces are concerned, however, the procedure used for backyard gardens can be followed. The main problem is the lack of leaves that normally make up the bulk of a compost heap. However, a little ingenuity can come to the rescue. One or two jumbo-sized plastic bags filled with leaves (donated only too happily by friends with trees) can easily be brought up to the terrace and put into the compost bin. Leaves are light to carry, so there would be little inconvenience. Some clever people have even been known to use these same plastic bags as containers for the compost by sticking holes in them for drainage (use two bags together for extra strength), or, if you want to be terribly chic about it, insert the plastic bags into large wooden tubs or whiskey barrels. But before you start any compost pile, think carefully whether it's worth all the trouble. It may be the "in" thing to do nowadays, but unless you have uses for those quantities of leaf mold that warrant the work and the space it takes, skip it. It's only for backyard gardens and large terraces. Others can do nicely with a small store-bought package of leaf mold once a year.

31. TRY A FEW VEGETABLES

Who can deny the taste thrill of eating really fresh vegetables— especially when you've lovingly grown them yourself? City dwellers are even more conscious of this, as they are accustomed to vegetables trucked in from faraway places (thereby losing much of their just-picked flavor) as well as to prices, which are getting higher by the hour. Where gardeners previously concentrated on flowers and other ornamental plants, they are now making room for vegetable gardens. The city dweller is caught up in this enthusiasm and wants to have a go at it himself. He hears tales of people growing fantastic crops of vegetables on their rooftops, giving away their surplus to lucky friends. Can it really be done?

Let's first deal with the negative points. Vegetables need sun in order to grow—at least six hours of it. Some vegetables can grow in what is called "partial shade," but this still means that a certain amount of sun is needed during the day. Leafy vegetables such as lettuce and cabbage can take more shade than root vegetables (radishes, beets), which in turn tolerate far more shade than vegetable fruit plants such as cucumbers, tomatoes and peppers, which require maximum sun. Very few backyard gardens in the heart of a large city get six hours or more of sun each day, so most attempts at a vegetable garden would have disappointing results. Gardens located near the city limits fare better, since there are usually few high-rise apartment buildings nearby to block out the sun. Terraces and penthouses are also better off, since the higher they are located, the greater the amount and intensity of the sun.

Space is another negative point. This is true of backyard garden plots as well as of terraces. To grow vegetables that will yield only an occasional plateful to the family is a waste of time, energy and valuable space. The space allocated to vegetables should be sufficiently large and well planned to yield worthwhile results. Allowance must be made for failures, which in a large garden are taken in stride and indeed fully expected, but this can be a great disappointment in a mini-sized plot. It's far better to concentrate on one or two vegetables which will give you a generous yield than to plant many kinds. You don't want to have to count the number of peas allowed on each dinner plate.

Attitude is a key factor. If you want to grow vegetables for the fun of it, even if all you get are two eggplants and four tomatoes, and you're thrilled beyond words at the achievement, then by all means do it. I'm the first to admit that it's an experience one shouldn't miss. I once gave a friend with a terrace one of my "cherry" tomato plants. He nurtured it, talked to it, lovingly attended to its needs. He gleefully reported to me at the end of the summer that he had had six of the miniature tomatoes and that to prolong the enjoyment, he and his wife had cut each tiny tomato in half before eating it. Now, wasn't it worth it to him?

However, if you're serious about growing vegetables for the sake of saving money at the supermarket and for summer-long fresh-picked taste, careful planning is in order. To know the pitfalls is to avoid them. The first thing to consider is where you will grow the vegetables. Regular beds are best, naturally, but how many get six hours of sun daily, and how many can be spared at the expense of ornamental plants? If you can't bring the sun to the bed, bring the bed to the sun, via portable containers that can be placed anywhere. Any container is suitable so long as it has the proper drainage holes and is at least a foot deep and as wide—the wider the better.

Wood boxes or attractive planters are excellent if the vegetables are going to be grown in full view; so are ordinary half-bushel or bushel baskets—their rustic, country look is in keeping with what is grown in them, and you can proudly point to a row of them as your "vegetable patch." If looks don't matter you can use all kinds of plastic containers, such as pails, baskets and garbage cans. (Always remember to drill drainage holes, four to six of them depending on the size of the container, about one-fourth inch wide, along the sides near the bottom of the container. Space them evenly all around.) The more plants you want to grow, the more containers you will need. Keep that in mind when you're making your list.

Good, ordinary soil is best for growing vegetables, neither overly sandy nor too heavy (the latter usually being found in backyard gardens). The soil should be loose and well enriched with humus and should have good drainage. Rake a 5-10-5 fertilizer into the soil and you're all set for planting. If you want some "fast-cropping," give a liquid feeding to the plants once a week with a soluble plant food such as 23-19-17 RA-PID-GRO.

Equally good results have been obtained by growing vegetables in synthetic soil, but it should be remembered that a *regularly* scheduled fertilizing program must be followed, since no natural soil nutrients are available to the plants. Its light weight is the chief attraction of soilless mixtures for terrace dwellers. A good mixture is: one bushel of horticultural grade vermiculite, one bushel of shredded peat moss, one and one-fourth cups of ground limestone, one-half cup of 20-percent superphosphate and one cup of 5-10-5 fertilizer. Mix all the ingredients thoroughly. Apply a teaspoon of the fertilizer per square foot of soil every three weeks once the plants start growing and showing at least two true leaves.

The next step is deciding which vegetables to grow. Space limits the city gardener: zucchini is easy to grow, has beautiful flowers and leaves and indeed is a highly ornamental plant, but it takes an enormous amount of space; even country gardeners limit themselves to a few. Rhubarb is not only a perennial and most attractive —but alas, also super-generous in size. However, the most popular vegetables require relatively little space. Listed below are those that will also grow in containers. Many new dwarf varieties of vegetables have been developed in the past few years and are made to order for city dwellers. Be on the lookout for them in your seed catalogs. Some examples: Dwarf Morden cabbage, Minnesota Midget cantaloupe, Tom Thumb lettuce, Tiny Tim tomatoes, Little Midget or Lollipop watermelon, Lady Finger potato, Gold Midget corn and so forth.

> BEETS. Tolerate some shade. Sow seeds as early in the spring as the ground can be worked. Wait until plants are six to eight inches high to thin them, and then stand them two to three inches apart. Keep making additional sowings to ensure a continuous supply. Then harvest when they're one to two inches in diameter.
>
> CARROTS. Will take some shade. Sow seeds in early spring. Thin plants so that they're two to three inches apart. Keep making additional sowings to ensure a continuous supply. Harvest when they're about one inch in diameter.
>
> CUCUMBERS. Need full sun and hot weather. Wait until all danger of frost has passed to sow seeds. Grow only one plant to a container (sow a few seeds but keep only the strongest seedling). Stake the plant or, better yet, train it on a trellis like a vine; it's an attractive plant with pretty flowers. It tastes best when picked while small. Protect

plant under a paper bag during cool nights when it's first set out.

EGGPLANT. Needs full sun. Set plants out when all danger of frost is past. Grow one plant to a container. Harvest when they're mature and glossy.

LEAF LETTUCE. Will take some shade. Sow seeds in early spring when the ground can be worked. Depending on the variety grown, thin seedlings from six to ten inches apart. Keep making additional sowings for a continuous supply. Lettuce is a cool-weather crop and won't grow in hot weather unless you buy special heat-resistant varieties. Grow "Ruby" lettuce for its ornamental value (a rich red color) as well as its taste. To harvest, cut the larger outer leaves or pull out the entire head. Some varieties will keep on growing new leaves as you cut off their outer ones for eating.

PEPPERS. Need full sun and hot weather. Grow one plant to a container. Wait until all danger of frost has passed before setting them out.

RADISHES. Will take some shade. They like cold weather but can't stand heat. Sow as early in the spring as possible regardless of frost. Thin them to one inch apart. Make several quick sowings before warm weather starts, and start again in the fall a month before the first frost is expected. Harvest when they're one-half to one inch in diameter.

SWISS CHARD. Will take some shade and tolerates hot weather. Sow very early in the spring. Thin plants four to five inches apart. Some plants can be harvested all summer long, since new leaves grow where outer ones are cut off for eating. Harvest when leaves are three to four inches long.

TOMATOES. Need full sun and warm weather. Grow one plant per container. Don't set the plants out until all danger of frost is gone. Dwarf varieties such as Burpee's "Pixie" or Park's "Tiny Tim" produce heavy crops of delicious, small tomatoes.

HERBS. Most herbs, being of Mediterranean origin, need full sun. They take a long time to grow from seed and success is by no means assured, so it's best to buy potted plants of those varieties most frequently used: parsley, chives, sweet basil, tarragon, rosemary, thyme and oregano. All these, except parsley and sweet basil, can be wintered over if given some protection in colder areas. They prefer ordinary, well-drained, sandy soil, on the alkaline side (which rules out most backyards unless the herbs are grown in containers). In fact, if the soil is on the poor side, the aroma of the leaves is intensified. (Let's be thankful for the breaks Nature gives us!) Depending on how much you need, grow herbs in individual pots or group three in one large container.

IMPORTANT NOTE: While it may give you a special feeling of accomplishment to grow all your own vegetables from seed, it's not always wise or possible. To get a head start on the season, and therefore a longer crop period, buy as many vegetable transplants as are available. These are seedlings already well grown and ready to be planted in your garden. Tomatoes, peppers and eggplants make the most successful seedlings. Starting vegetables in flats indoors, from seed, is not for the apartment dweller. Few window sills have enough space to hold flats (low rectangular wooden boxes) and to provide protection from drainage. Buy healthy, sturdy plants and give yourself a break. You'll have enough other obstacles to overcome if you're looking for challenges.

Always read directions on the seed packages carefully and *follow them.* They reflect years of research on the part of the grower, and he *wants* you to succeed. His business depends on it.

32. KNOW YOUR ENEMIES

The country gardener has nothing on his city counterpart when it comes to obstacles to gardening. Consider high winds, scorching sun and air pollution added to the usual breeds of pests and plant diseases. A city gardener faces all these challenges, and yet there is no need to be discouraged. Although there may be no cures in sight (we can't yet change the weather), there are ways of coping with these problems and minimizing their damage to plants.

Wind

While stagnant air is prevalent in most backyard gardens, squeezed as they are at the bottoms of skyscraper canyons, savage winds rage around terraces—the higher the terrace, the greater the wind velocity. I recall only too vividly one windy, early spring day when, while I was taking measurements on a client's twentieth-floor terrace overlooking Central Park, a furious gust of wind swept across the enormous terrace (it had four exposures!), nearly knocking me down. I was really frightened and raced back to indoor safety. The terrace was newly acquired and totally bare, giving the wind full rein to sweep down in all its might. But whether small or large, terraces are windy places and this accounts for the majority of plant losses each year.

Most high-rise dwellers do not consider wind an enemy of plants, no doubt thinking how pleasant it is to feel some of that breeze on a hot summer day when the rest of the city is sweltering. However, people do not stay on the terrace all night, all through the year, summer and winter—and if the going gets too rough, they quickly retreat inside their cozy apartments. Not so the plants. Shrubs and trees have to take the weather on a permanent basis and it's no joke for them.

Before the terrace gardener spends one dollar on his plants, he should install some sort of fencing if he doesn't already have any. Sometimes the small terrace, which is really little more than a balcony, has an open space below the railing or parapet through which the wind sweeps, not only on plants but up the legs of people as well. Bamboo screening attached to the railing helps to cut this down. Kept natural or sprayed a flat white, bamboo is an attractive backdrop for floor planters or boxes attached to the railing. If the terrace has neighbors on either side, fencing may be already taken care of, if for no other reason than privacy. If there are no neighbors, a sapling fence is in order to block off the wind. (Obviously you should know which way the wind blows in your area, for perhaps a fence on only one side is sufficient.) Grow a vine up the fence or place a tall, airy shrub in front of it.

If there is a spectacular view and it means a great deal to you to be able to enjoy it while in a reclining position, glass panels are the best solution. They're expensive and obviously only recommended for small areas, where admiring the view gets top priority in the pleasure the owners derive from their terrace. Because glass provides both protection from wind and visibility, it's a popular screening choice with beach clubs and seaside houses.

For others, there are many types of fences available in a wide price range, much of the cost depending on availability of the material in that part of the country. Stockade fencing made of woven saplings is by far the most popular style. Whatever the type of wood fencing used, it should not have an airtight, solid surface. This prevents the fence from "giving" in a high wind, and it will most certainly be knocked down. A slight space left between posts is all that is necessary to allow the wind to pass through, thereby reducing its destructiveness. Planting a hedge or placing tubs of shrubs in front of such a fence gives further protection from the wind and forms a handsome backdrop for flowers. Where this is not feasible, growing a vine up the fence will be equally attractive.

Another way of reducing wind velocity on larger terraces is with "islands" or "peninsula" planting, built-in planters or tubs in the center of the terrace or at right angles to the wall. Plant these with shrubs and an evergreen ground cover, as well as spring bulbs and summer annuals for color. One or more "islands" visually break up the "plaza" look of a large terrace, creating design interest and more intimate seating arrangements—but more important, they stop the wind in its tracks, forcing it to detour, thereby sharply cutting down its "bite."

An awning or some sort of overhead protection is another method of frustrating the wind. An awning, however, is only useful for this purpose during the summer months, since it's not used in winter for the very reason that the wind would tear it to shreds. An awning is not a permanent solution to year-round protection of trees and shrubs, but it does help with summer flowers, hanging baskets and house plants summering outdoors. If there is a terrace directly over yours, this automatically provides protection from above. In the case of large penthouses and rooftops, a permanent, attractive wood pergola is a handsome solution to the wind problem. It also provides room for hanging baskets and vines. In the winter, shrubs of "borderline" hardiness can be placed under the pergola for shelter. Even though its roof is not a solid surface, thereby allowing the wind to pass through it, its lath-like design offers enough obstacles to reduce the wind velocity.

After fencing and an overhead structure have been considered, the terrace gardener should next turn his attention to the careful selection of appropriate plants. This is of crucial importance. Some plants hate wind, others don't care one bit. (Pines and junipers don't mind the wind, but some broad-leaved evergreens do.) Learn to know which is which, and don't let any salesman talk you into buying a plant that is attractive but not wind-hardy. You'll only have to replace it in a year or two. (Annuals are exceptions, as they must be replaced each year.) Plants that grow by the seashore and are accustomed to fierce winds are ideal for high terraces and rooftops. You *know* they'll make it for you if they can take the fury of a rocky ocean site. As with any type of gardening in a problem area, high-rise gardening is also a perpetual lesson in humility and self-control. We don't grow what *we* want to grow as much as what nature *lets* us grow. The real success in gardening is to adapt to the environment—not to fight it and impose our own wishes. Forget growing your favorite delphiniums on the fiftieth floor—buy a good print of them instead and hang it in the living room.

Sun

Cities never get as cold as the countryside, but they certainly get a lot hotter. The sun bouncing off concrete pavements and skyscrapers is intensified to an alarming degree and is trapped there sometimes for several days without relief. Backyard gardens, with their usually excessive shade, get the heat but not the actual rays of the sun; terraces get the full brunt of both. Burned, dried-up, cooked plants are a familiar complaint of the high-rise gardener, especially if he faces south or west. However, here again there are ways of minimizing the harm done by excessive sun.

The first and most sensible course of action is the proper selection of plants. As with wind-hardy plants, there are sun-loving ones; those that are happy by the sea are going to be equally so on a sun-drenched terrace. Forget wild flowers and others found in woodlands. There are so many plants which not only like the sun but require it for healthy growth and prolific blooming that sensible selection is no problem. Those plants that are "border-line" cases can be placed out of direct sun during the summer months, or at the base of broad, bushy shrubs.

Mulch everything in sight to keep roots cool: trees, shrubs, annuals, perennials, whether they are in containers (all the more reason) or planted directly in beds. Apply the mulch at least three inches thick after you've watered the soil deeply or after a heavy rain. Water plants regularly and copiously thereafter. Overhead misting with the hose also helps to cool off plants and create needed humidity. Hose the flooring of the terrace while you're at it. A bonus here is that you will also have washed off the day's accumulation of soot on plants and flooring. We all know how much cooler it is on the grass than on the pavement on a hot summer day, and so it is with terraces. A wide expanse of un-interrupted flooring with smallish flower beds not only looks hotter, but actually is. It's much cooler to reverse the plan. If yours is an unusually sunny terrace, increase the size and/or num-ber of planters, even if all you put in them are ground covers. It'll at least be green and cool-looking—as well as maintenance-free. Have a fountain or a pool with recirculating water to increase hu-midity in the area as well as to add a soothing, cooling effect that only trickling water can create.

Heat bounces off bare walls, so cover them with ivy or some other kind of vine. (Baltic ivy is hardier than English ivy.) In short, to reduce damage from the sun, have as much greenery as possible, keep bare flooring to a minimum, provide shade through trees and overhead structures, mist plants as often as possible, deeply mulch all plant material to hold the moisture and coolness within the soil and only buy plants that thrive in the sun.

Air Pollution

Whether we are sixteen or sixty, we all know about air pollution, for we can't help but be aware of what damage it does to both human and plant life and that it is one more negative by-product of so-called progress. Plants are actually more sensitive to some air pollutants than are animals and man because plants haven't as much tissue between the biochemically active cells and the external atmosphere. Man and animals generally have more tissue. Because of this sensitivity, plants are often used as monitors for such pollutants as hydrocarbons, carbon monoxide, sulfur oxides, and particulates (soot, smoke, dust). Hydrocarbons and hydrogen oxides interact, with the aid of the sun, to form other pollutants typical of smog. Most cities now have primary air quality standards designed to protect human health and have passed secondary standards to cover plant life.

For a gardener, little can be done with air pollution other than coping with it, although as a private citizen, one can voice concern through supporting those who are working to bring it under control and to reduce it to a negligible degree. But in the meantime, air pollution is part of urban living and we must make the best of it. Pollution affects plants both internally and externally, and it takes a knowing, experienced eye to know whether plant damage is caused by pollution or by some more conventional enemy. In acute cases, there is severe visible damage to the leaf tissue, resembling a burn, or loss of some of the chlorophyll. More frequent is chronic damage to the plant, which occurs over a long period of time and is hard to diagnose. *Too much* sulfur dioxide affects the margins and tips of leaves and between the veins, while fluoride is also reflected in damage to the edges and tips of the leaves (gladioli and iris are very sensitive to fluoride). Smog, originating from many oxidants, makes its mark through silvering or bronzing on the underside of the leaf. (Petunias are most sensitive to auto exhaust and carnations to ethylene.)

However, some pollutants act as fertilizers for plants and can be termed beneficial. Atmospheric ammonia and sulfur dioxide, in *low* concentrations, supply nitrogen and sulfur to plants.

Gardeners shouldn't attempt to diagnose air pollution effects on plants, but rather should concentrate on those plants that can "take it," as shown by the ones that survive year after year in large urban areas. Frequent—at least daily—showering of the plants helps to wash away much of the pollution. Local newspapers report areas within cities that are most polluted, so act accordingly when misting plants: the more polluted your area, the more frequently you should take to the hose. Keep an alert eye for what grows well around you; your next-door neighbors have successes and failures also. Get acquainted with their hardy "achievers."

Coping, adapting and experimenting are all any gardener can do when faced with the urban enemies of gardening. Wind, sun and air pollution all produce a "survival of the fittest" situation among plants, which learn to adapt far better than we give them credit for. Enough trees have "made it" to give us the shade our gardens need, sufficient flowers succeed in providing us with color and we have many shrubs to choose from. It's only a matter of sticking with the winners—and pampering them while they're valiantly putting up the fight.

Pests and Diseases

Preventive measures are the best against plant pests and diseases. This means good housekeeping outdoors, as true of city gardening as in the country. Pests and diseases don't thrive when plants are well-spaced with plenty of room for good air circulation; when a diseased or damaged limb is removed the moment it's spotted; when weeds are kept under control; when debris is picked up and the garden cleaned after a storm; when fertilizers are used as needed; when the soil is kept in good, friable, loose condition which helps plants grow strong and healthy. In short, pests and disease don't like a garden that's neat, tidy and well cared for.

I am not among those who turn purple at the mere mention of the word pesticides. They are the farmer's allies when used with discretion and *knowledge*. But in the city, I feel strongly that their use should be discouraged, except in extreme cases. City gardens are so close together, with people and pets always nearby, that the use of pesticides is far more dangerous than in the country where open spaces offer some protection and dilution of the chemicals' potency—although even in the country judicious use of chemicals is a must.

A gardener should know *why* he's using a certain pesticide, as well as *how* and *when* to use it properly. Simply to spray plants as a preventive measure or because a few insects have been spotted is both foolish and dangerous. The aim of pest control is just that: control, not eradication. The latter is virtually impossible anyway.

Try the safest methods first: pick off by hand any pests or tell-tale traces you can see—such as galls, "cotton" balls, rolled-up leaves (with the pest curled up inside)—and drop them into a coffee can with some kerosene in it. Where feasible, wash the plant with a solution of soap and warm water. If it's a small pot, turn it upside down and dunk the plant in the soapy solution, first covering the soil with aluminum wrap. In the case of larger plants, use a sponge to wash off the affected areas. Rinse with the hose or a sponge dipped in clear water. Snip off all faded flowers—a job that would be ridiculous in a country garden, but within the confines of a small city backyard or terrace it's not such a laborious task. Carry a plastic bag as you make your daily rounds and pick off these dead blooms. It keeps the beds neat and prevents pests and diseases. Turning a strong stream of water on a shrub (not the more delicate flowers) can sometimes be sufficient to control the pests.

A relaxed attitude is also necessary. Simply because a tree or a shrub has a few yellow or speckled leaves or some other imperfection doesn't mean that it's about to conk out. People aren't perfect either. We get pimples, we get colds, we lose some hair—none of it means that it's serious and that we're about to depart from this world. So why rush to grab an insecticide can and spray the plant silly? Only plastic plants have every leaf absolutely smooth, evenly green, shiny—in other words, sheer perfection—and that's why they can be spotted so easily as artificial plants. Nature has flaws, and that's the charm of it. Resort to chemicals only when absolutely necessary. In the case of large trees, have a professional tree doctor diagnose the ailment and take the necessary steps.

There are other reasons for not spraying unnecessarily. Air pollution is enough of a problem without adding any more toxic ingredients into the air we breathe. Small children love to pull off a leaf and chew on it. (So do adults, but they're usually wise enough to engage in this highly satisfying pleasure in the wide-open countryside.) Birds and animals not only eat some plants or berries (cats especially have a penchant for grass) but also drink from small puddles of water which may be polluted with insecticide.

Still another reason is on a broader scale. Our generation is conscious of the worldwide famine among underdeveloped countries. The raising of crops, for these people, is not for ornamental purposes but for sheer survival. They need to fight nature's obstacles with man's weapons of fertilizers and pesticides which save crops in order to feed hungry people. I'm not advocating that you let your prize azalea die to avoid using a chemical—but I am suggesting that the desire for perfection in plants should take a secondary place to more serious motives. Naturally, if you are going to show off your plants in a garden tour or horticultural show and everything has to be super-magnificent, it's a different story. But few people garden for such reasons.

An entire book could be written on the subject of plant pests and diseases, and indeed some excellent ones have been (see the bibliography). Several shelves could be cleared just for storing chemicals of all sorts—each one for a different bug or disease. Articles in newspapers and magazines about the numerous enemies we have lurking around the garden ready to do our plants in, and the right chemical to use on each one, boggle the mind. Actually, a few products are all that are needed as a last resort, if the proper sanitary measures already discussed fail to control the pests. The important thing is to trap the culprits *before* they have had a chance to multiply to dizzying proportions and cause damage accordingly.

Know the enemy, but there's no need to get too involved. After all, most city gardeners have only a few shrubs, a tree or two and flowers, plus a patch of lawn, maybe, and/or a ground cover. There is no need to arm yourself with a plant pathologist's knowledge. Basically, there are two major categories of insects: those that chew the plants and those that suck the juices out of them.

Chewing insects include beetles, caterpillars, leaf-miners, sawflies and borers. They leave signs of their chewing behind them— piles of sawdust, bitten leaves, holes. The trick is to control them by picking them off or, failing this, by poisoning what they eat (the plant in this case), but obviously without killing the plant. This explains why careful measurement of the chemical is essential. This is true with *any* chemical.

The sucking insects are many—aphids, lace bugs, leafhoppers, thrips, spider mites and scale insects. They puncture the surface of the plant and then suck out the juices. The leaves turn yellow, curling around the pests, and there's a sticky substance on the surface of the leaf. Pinching off the entire curled leaf is the way to control them, but barring this, the only control is direct spraying on their bodies—not too easy a job, as it must be done on the underside of the leaf to be effective.

You could get away, therefore, with one insecticide for each of these two insect categories (such as rotenone for chewing insects and pyrethrum for sucking ones; both insecticides are of low toxicity to mammals, but rotenone is lethal to fish). There are many other chemicals available, some more toxic than others. Fortunately, we have alert laws in many states covering safe use of insecticides by the home gardener.

Dormant oils are good for certain sucking insects (scales) but must be applied in early spring only, and when the temperature is above 40 degrees. Check the labels to make sure that the one you're using will not harm the trees in your garden. For very small jobs, aerosols are effective, although too expensive for large properties. Systemics are insecticides that kill sucking insects by going through the plant's system, so that when the insects suck on the stems and leaves it kills them—but not the plant.

When it comes to diseases of plants, the outlook is gloomy for the nonprofessional. There are so many types of diseases that only an expert can tell exactly what is ailing the plant. Most of the time the expert will advise you to throw the plant out. The virus, fungus or bacterial disease that the plant may have is not only killing it but can destroy those surrounding it. When it's obvious that the culprit is not an insect, then it's a disease, and it's better to face the loss of the plant.

Plant disease can be avoided by watering carefully in the early morning in backyard gardens (these gardens take longer to dry), by providing adequate light and air circulation around plants and by proper drainage. Buy disease-resistant plants (more and more are now available) and destroy immediately any branch or twig that appears sickly. Watch for any mildew, black spot, wilting, tumors, dwarfing and mottled yellowing of the plant. You can buy or make your own all-purpose spray, consisting of a combination insecticide-fungicide-miticide, and let one spray do the job of three. Read labels carefully, as they tell you which chemicals are compatible with which others and how much to use of each.

A few words of precaution:

Always read the directions carefully before mixing the preparation and using it.

Keep special containers, measuring cups and spoons, for the use of chemicals only, and place them out of reach of children and pets. This goes double for the chemicals themselves.

Don't spray when there are people or pets around, or when the wind is stiff and can turn the spray right back in your face or your neighbor's face.

Wraparound sunglasses are great to prevent spray from hitting your eyes. Don't get any of the chemical on your skin. If you do, wash it off right away with soap and water.

If you use a chemical in powder form, cover your mouth and nose with a scarf or the gauze-type mask you buy at drugstores when a child has a cold and you don't want to have it spread to the entire family.

Don't sit out in the garden for several hours after spraying. The still air in a backyard keeps the chemicals in the same spot for quite a while. On a terrace, the wind is a help for once. By dispersing the fumes rapidly, it prevents concentration of dangerous chemicals. Needless to add, don't spray if the next-door neighbors are sitting on their terrace or patio.

Treat chemicals with great respect, because they are all poisonous to one degree or another. You're better off not using any, but if you must, please follow manufacturer's directions and cautions.

Pets

Pets are certainly not our enemies, unless, of course, it happens to be the neighbor's St. Bernard in our petunia bed. The average center-of-town backyard garden is usually—and certainly should be—totally and securely fenced in, not only to keep out neighbor-

CHEMICALS	WHAT THEY CONTROL	HOW TO APPLY
All-purpose rose mixture (contains insecticide, miticide, fungicide)	Black spot and mildew. For just a few rose bushes, it's best to buy an all-purpose mixture already done for you. You can use Benlate alone in late summer for extra mildew control.	Spray every two weeks, starting in May, through September.
Benlate (benomyl)	A good fungicide against powdery mildew of ornamental plants.	Follow instructions on label.
Borerkil (a lindane paste)	Borers are at work when you see sawdust coming out of lilacs and other ornamentals.	Squirt into the holes in June.
Cygon (dimethoate) (also has systemic action)	Holly leaf miners (small black flies when adult). Rhododendron, azalea and hawthorn lace bugs and for pyracantha. Bugs infest leaves in full sun.	Spray in May. Meta-systemic R may also be used. Spray in June. Can also use carbaryl, malathion or diazinon.
Dacthal	Anti-crabgrass pre-emergent control for lawns. Other substitutes are Siduron (tupersan), Betasan (bensulide) or Balan (benefin).	Apply in early spring, since these products are not effective once weeds are already growing.
Doom	A milky disease spore powder that kills Japanese Beetle grubs. Use only once. Is slow to act, so patience is necessary.	Apply in September and only if no other insecticide is used at this time.
Kelthane (dicofol)	A miticide against spider mites (look for dull leaves, tiny specks or webs on evergreens, phlox and other ornamentals, especially on terraces.	Spray in June. Tedio and rotenone may also be used instead.
Malathion or Cythion (has a less offensive odor)	For sucking insects. Pyrethrum may be substituted. Scales—yellow crawlers on euonymus and pines. Aphids—found on flowers. Leafhoppers—look for burned leaf margins turned under on dahlias and others. Thrips—dust gladiolus corms before storing.	Spray in June in addition to a dormant oil. Spray in July. Spray in July. Dust in October.

CHEMICALS	WHAT THEY CONTROL	HOW TO APPLY
Metaldehyde	Bait to kill slugs. Try a dish of stale beer first. They'll crawl in and drown. Chances are that this will work better than the metaldehyde!	Apply late in the day when you spot them.
Methyl arsonates	Crabgrass and other grassy weeds *after* they've appeared.	Apply as directed on label. Can also use Ansar, Sodar, Crab-E-Rad.
Pyrethrum	For sucking insects (aphids, lace bugs, scale insects, mites).	Use as directed.
Rotenone	For chewing insects (beetles, caterpillars, leaf-miners, borers). A safe insecticide made from the roots of a plant in Peru. It's highly toxic to fish, but of low toxicity to mammals.	Use as directed.
Sevin (carbaryl)	For chewing insects like the following: Caterpillars (nests swelling—at tips of twigs). Andromeda lace bugs.	Spray in April. Spray in May—can also use Malathion.
	European pine sawfly—larvae eat old needles on pines. Leaf miners—leaf blotches on birches.	Spray in May. Spray in May—Malathion can also be substituted.
	Japanese beetles on flowers. Chinch bugs—create brown patches in lawns that are in full sun.	Spray in July. Treat in August. Aspon can also be used.
Miscellaneous	*Fumigants* are dangerous to use. Best to stay away from these types of chemicals. If you must treat a particular spot in your garden, try PCNB, sold as "Terraclor," one tablespoon per gallon of water. Pull out and destroy rotted plants first. Cut off and burn any brown tips or needles on pines and junipers. Hand-pick and burn bagworms in winter, since the pest in the egg-stage winters over in the bags.	

ing pets, but for safety and privacy as well. This takes care of dogs but not cats, whose climbing skills are legendary. Fortunately, cats are light-footed and small and do little damage to shrubbery. They move slowly (unless chased by dogs or energetic boys), more interested in sniffing everything than in destroying. However, this doesn't mean that one won't settle for a doze in the middle of your flower bed. Be philosophical. There's little you can do unless you want to keep a constant watch or put up a charged electric fence.

When it comes to your *own* dog, there are two things you should do. First, take it out for its walks just as you would if you didn't have a garden. This will exercise the dog so that he won't take out his excess energy on your patio and will also ensure that your garden won't turn into his outdoor privy. Trees and shrubs can take it, but flowers can be damaged by a frisky dog, so have raised beds for your flowers instead of planting them at ground level. It goes without saying that a large dog can jump over the raised planter, but it most definitely is a deterrent. This is true for small children also.

In some large cities, one occasionally finds "communal" gardens. This phenomenon occurs when a block of private houses on two streets, back to back, does away with individual fencing, preferring one large, shared, park-like garden. You cultivate that part which is your own property, and share in the cost of a gardener to take care of path maintenance, tree pruning and so forth. This arrangement appeals to certain people, but if your neighbors have pets, you're in big trouble. There's nothing to prevent their dogs from entering your property and doing precisely what they choose. A friend of mine in New York City, whose private house is part of such an arrangement, is still trying to figure out a solution after more than twenty years. Even if you speak to your neighbors (risking future friction and frostiness), what can *they* do about restraining their dog's activities, short of keeping him on a leash?

The problem is also shared by city houses away from the heart of town, separated one from the other by narrow alleyways leading to the garage in the rear. Pets roam freely and there's nothing you can do about it. Raised beds with border fences will keep out small dogs, but they present little challenge to the big ones. There are animal repellents available in spray cans or rope form that you lay on the ground as a barrier; however, one good shower destroys much of their effectiveness, so that can become pretty much of an ongoing job.

If your flower beds are seriously damaged each year, you might try container gardening. Stick with shrubs and ground covers for ground-level beds, but plant your annuals in large containers grouped attractively around the garden. This method is as dog-proof as you can get.

Terrace owners are solidly fenced in, so there's no problem with neighbors' pets. When it comes to your own, follow the advice given to the backyard gardener. Terraces rely on containers much more than do house gardens, so the problem is more easily solved. But make sure the containers are high and large enough. Small pots are easily knocked over by a dog who thinks it's fun jumping over them.

Little tots are tough to control, but then children that small shouldn't be left unattended anyway. A few no-nos when they're first caught pulling out a pretty flower should, one hopes, get the message across. But don't count on it.

When my husband and I first bought our weekend place in the country ten years ago, we were forever chasing large dogs from our garden. (Of course we thought that the *wild* creatures, such as foxes and deer, were cute, but then they're exotic compared with dogs!) A wise friend of ours, a long-time dedicated gardener who happened to be visiting us as we were going through our dog-chasing routine, summed it up simply and beautifully and we haven't bothered since. All he said was: "Together with the weather, there's nothing you can do about dogs and children in a garden."

Welcome birds, for they are a delightful addition to any garden. The number you will get, if any, depends on many factors: your location within the city (a large park nearby, density of traffic in your area, noise, pollution, etc.), the kinds of plants you grow (trees and tall shrubs offer protection and nesting places, and those bearing berries in the fall provide tempting food) and how high you are if yours is a terrace garden. Keeping your bird feeders filled and providing a basin of water further entices birds to linger in your garden. How many birds visit you is often an amusing topic of conversation at a party, an opportunity for one-upmanship like fishermen's tales. If one claims to have birds on his ninth-floor terrace, there's bound to be somebody who'll quickly reply that *he* gets them on his fifteenth-floor penthouse.

33. A LITTLE NIGHT LIGHTING FOR DRAMA

Whether or not to light your garden at night depends on several factors. First, do you use the terrace after dark frequently enough to make it worthwhile? When you entertain, do you herd everybody indoors when the sun sets or does the party continue outdoors, weather permitting? Will your local building codes permit outdoor electrical wiring underground? And last, consider the cost factor. Landscape lighting can run into sizable sums of money for both materials and labor.

If having a garden in the city is one of your joys and is a major reason for keeping you from moving out to the suburbs, there is no denying that even the simplest lighting will add an extra dimension to the garden, extending its use and allowing you to derive still greater pleasure from it. If it's a high-rise terrace, outdoor lights are already built in for you as part of the building construction. But you might wish to highlight a particularly handsome tree, a tiered fountain or a flower bed. If it's a backyard garden, there's also the lighting of steps if the garden is on two or more levels, and the lighting of the terrace area where you sit and dine, as well as the barbecue itself if you use one (you should see what you're cooking and what you're eating) and any especially decorative features such as statuary or a specimen shrub.

Before planning any type of lighting, it's good to know what is available to do what job.

1. *Low, widespread lighting.* This is mounted on or in the ground and is used for lighting paths, steps and low flowers. Fixtures resemble mushrooms or bells and are from twelve to fourteen inches high. The twenty-five- to forty-watt lamps are gracefully concealed (as they should be under *all* circumstances) with the light reflecting *downward.*

Artificial lighting serves a dual purpose: It highlights trees and shrubbery ▶ and also lights the path leading to the door. Experiment before permanently installing the lighting.
General Electric Company

2. *High, widespread lighting.* The facts for low lighting apply here too, except that the fixtures are from thirty inches to six feet tall. The light is also spread *downward.* These fixtures are used to light taller flower beds, tops of steps, etc. Care must be exercised to ensure proper scale; the stem of the fixture should not stick up too far above whatever it is illuminating.

3. *Low, horizontal lighting.* The fixtures are very low but the light is projected in a *horizontal* plane, to the sides, neither down nor up. Lamps are hidden from view by attractive reflectors (frequently shaped like leaves or rocks). These fixtures are good for outlining an entire flower bed by creating a contour effect, or for lighting rock gardens.

4. *Wide-beam uplighting.* Floodlights or fluorescent fixtures are mounted in the ground or on a pole to light a wide area of plantings. Equipment must be located where it can be hidden by shrubbery. The beam is aimed *upward.*

5. *Controlled uplighting.* This is used primarily to highlight the shape of a tree. The lamp is shielded so that the narrow beam is aimed *upward.* It can be hidden in the shrubbery or in the crotch of the tree.

6. *Wide-beam downlighting.* Use the decorative lantern types to focus general light over outdoor table and chairs. The light shines *downward.*

7. *Controlled downlighting.* Narrow beams of light are aimed *downward* at the subject. Lamps are mounted on tree branches or ceilings of permanent overhead structures over terraces.

8. *General lighting.* Fixtures come in all sizes and shapes (globes, lanterns, bubbles, wall brackets) and are used for outdoor living areas, as opposed to garden areas, because the lamps are very bright—enough to read by in a pinch.

Making the best use of the vast equipment at your disposal requires study. Subtlety is the key word when planning any outdoor lighting. In the small garden, which means most backyards and terraces, concentrate on only one or two focal points in the *garden* itself (as opposed to the *living area* where you eat and sit, which requires its own type of lighting). The charm of night lighting is that it's mysterious, soft, fairy-tale-like, as if it came from moonbeams rather than man. But when using lights for safety or for purely functional reasons, don't be too subtle; your guests should be able to see the steps clearly and to distinguish a fork from a knife. And for the sake of protection, you should be able to floodlight the entire nearby area with the flick of one switch.

In using any kind of uplighting, care must be taken that the beam does not annoy neighbors. This is also true of floodlights. Enough flexibility is allowed from the vast equipment available to prevent problems with neighbors. After selecting a site for a fixture, experiment with the direction of its beam before final installation.

Selection of the proper light bulb is largely a matter of trial and error. Fixtures can often take more than one size and wattage of lamp. The distance between the fixture and the object to be lighted affects the type of bulb needed, as does the objective of the lighting in the first place. Bulbs come in a variety of colors. I prefer white, as I find the others garish and distorting, but this is purely a personal opinion.

Lighting fixtures should be installed by an electrical contractor. Far too much is involved for the layman to attempt to do it himself. Permanent wiring (which must be weatherproof) has to be run underground, be properly encased, have adequate drainage and protection, etc. No need to go into the rest of it—you get the general picture. The only outdoor lighting that can be done by just about anybody is the low-voltage type, of which there are several kinds available. This lighting operates with a six- to twelve-volt transformer, making it relatively safe to handle. The installation of the 120-volt wiring that leads to the transformer, however, has to be done by an electrician.

The popularity of low-voltage equipment (besides its low cost) is its simplicity: you run the cables to the spots you want lighted, burying each cable a couple of inches in the soil, which you can do even with a trowel (if my husband can do it, believe me, it's easy). The lamps are low, mounted on short spikes that you place where you choose. However, while this type of equipment has much merit, it obviously can't compare with the regular 120-volt equipment for versatility and for more sophisticated lighting.

Artifical lighting increases the hours you can enjoy your garden—whether it is in a backyard or a penthouse. Just a few carefully placed lamps can highlight trees, shrubs, borders, or statuary. Don't overdo it; a little goes a long way.
General Electric Company

The two photographs illustrate ways of directing light beams. Lamps should be as invisible as possible.
General Electric Company

34. HOW TO BUY PLANTS WISELY

When it comes to plants and gardening supplies, the city gardener is not nearly as fortunate as his suburban or country friends who have large nurseries and well-stocked garden centers at their disposal. On top of that, the city dweller has to pay more for everything because of the added transportation costs. On the bright side of the picture, however, is the fact that he needs very little in comparison to the demands of a country garden. Shrubs and annuals are the mainstays of city backyard and terrace gardens, with one or two trees if space permits, as well as a clump or two of perennials and a few spring bulbs. This is average, of course, between balconies that need less and spacious penthouses that can be as elaborately landscaped as any suburban estate. But by and large, the city gardener is so restricted in space that the amount of plant material required to create his green oasis is equally limited.

Buying plants wisely is the result of good planning. How to go about planning your garden has already been covered (see chapters 3 and 15), so you should have a very good idea of the kind and number of plants you need. Consult the charts listing the varieties of plants suitable for urban gardening, selecting the ones that most appeal to you (after all, gardening is a highly personal creative expression) as well as those appropriate for your location (backyard versus high-rise terrace).

When examining plants, always look for signs of new growth shown by the shiny, lighter green of the tiny leaves at the tips of stems. This way, at least you know that the plant is healthy, growing and producing new leaves or new shoots, not to mention flower buds. Stay away from plants that have dull, slightly droopy foliage. Size has little to do with vigor. A smallish plant covered with new growth is far healthier than a larger one showing signs of doing nothing.

It would be nice to say that you could trust all plant stores so completely that you shouldn't have to worry about pests or diseases in the plants, but sadly enough, this would be overly optimistic. Too much depends on *where* you buy your plants (more about that later). It doesn't do any harm to do a little checking yourself. Take a close look at the plant. (If you use glasses, for goodness' sake now is the time to put them on.) Look under the leaves and where the leaves join the stems. Do you spot any bugs? Do the leaves feel sticky to the touch, the way honey does? Is there a shiny substance on the leaves? Do you see what look like bits of fluffy cotton or tiny cobwebs? Are the leaves partially chewed or do they have holes in them? Any one of these signs spells trouble and the plant is best put back on its bench. Select another plant (after giving it the same once-over).

The shape of a plant is important—especially one that will be grown in a container, since it will be seen from all sides. It needn't be absolutely symmetrical (that's the beauty of nature versus artificial plants), but its branches and foliage should be fairly evenly distributed. Shrubs which are grown too closely together outdoors in large nurseries have sides that are pitifully bare, which may or may not ever fill out. A smaller specimen, well shaped and bushy all over, is more likely to continue growing in the same manner.

A stocky plant with several stems is a far better buy than a taller one with only one stem. In annuals especially, you get a greater display of flowers from plants with multiple stems. This is also true when buying vines. It's tempting to select the climbing vine with the one long trailing stem, but the one with three shorter stems is a smarter choice because you'll eventually get far more coverage.

Where to buy plants deserves serious consideration. If you have a car and can drive out to one of the better large nurseries in the surrounding countryside, by all means do so. The selection will be larger, the plants freshly dug and the prices lower. But with the recent increased interest in gardening, both indoors and outdoors (a result of deep concern for the ecology and nature in general), garden supply centers have invaded urban areas, so that the city dweller can now do his shopping right in town.

A distinction should be made between a nursery and a local florist or house-plant shop. A nursery sells trees and shrubs, in containers or balled and burlapped (often called B & B—the root ball is wrapped in burlap). The city gardener knows he's finally "arrived" when B & B no longer means simply a liqueur. The nursery also sells some of the more popular perennials, flats of annuals and vegetable transplants, not to mention supplies such as peat moss, potting soil, tools and so forth. A florist sells cut flowers and house plants, while other stores specialize only in house plants.

Some bargains in plant material exist, but bear in mind that you usually get what you pay for. It takes years and much experience to grow healthy, good-sized trees and shrubs. This is why you should patronize the best nursery in your area. You will be buying only a few major plants and they will be with you for many, many years, so start with good stock. A nursery is not here today and gone tomorrow; it depends on its good reputation to stay in business. Trucks parked at street corners selling shrubs and other plants are there one day, and are nowhere to be seen the next. Buy from them at your own risk!

Don't be afraid to ask the advice of the nurseryman at a nursery that grows its own plants as well as sells them, as is frequently the case in the country. Plants are like his children, and he won't stop talking about them and telling you which ones are best for your needs. Nurseries that are outlets for plants grown elsewhere can be very good as far as plant material is concerned, but forget it when it comes to advice. The salespeople may know no more than you do (and maybe less) about horticulture. However, there is usually one man, the owner or his assistant, who is knowledgeable, and if you can get his ear, he'll help you out.

But be definite about your preference. If, after consulting the charts on pages 87–99, you've decided that you need a flowering crab apple tree, two andromedas, a juniper and four flats of assorted annuals to round out your garden, stick with your list. His advice can help you decide *which* crab apple is best, *which* kind of juniper and the heights of the annuals when they are fully grown. Leaving everything up to the nurseryman is inviting him to get rid of his overstock. Sometimes a substitute is unavoidable, but be sure that it's in the same category, culture-wise, as your original choice. For example, if you wanted a shade-loving annual, don't settle for one that requires sun. If you have a terrace, don't substitute a shrub that won't tolerate wind.

Besides the local or country nursery, another source of plants is mail-order houses. These are unexcelled when it comes to obtaining out-of-the-ordinary plants that are usually not available locally. Perennials, dwarf shrubs, wild flowers, rock garden plants and water plants are among the many types that are best ordered by mail. Many of these firms specialize in a particular category of plants and have an astounding variety. They also have an impeccable reputation built over many years and furnish the necessary information for planting and growing their plants (see chapter 35).

Shipping techniques have so improved in recent years that there is little need to fear damage to plants sent through the mail. If there is any damage, and if the firm is promptly advised, it will usually replace the plant. One word of caution, however: plants purchased by mail are small. It's obviously easier and far less costly to ship young plants than heavy, mature ones. But you will be rewarded for your patience in the pleasure of watching them grow to maturity. Another plus is that younger plants adapt to a new and sometimes difficult environment far better than would older ones. (Don't we all!)

Mail-order catalogs list the size of each plant and the time of year when it may be expected to bloom if it's a flowering type. Detailed descriptions and/or photographs give you a good indication of the plant's growth habit and looks. Local nurseries dependent on large volume and rapid turnover do not find it economically sound, understandably, to carry rarer plants. This is where the mail-order houses take over, and we depend on them for nature's loveliest creations. A word of caution: some catalogs are little more than mimeographed pamphlets, and others are elaborately illustrated handbooks. Neither format is indicative of the quality of plants—merely of the size and volume of the nursery and the personal attitude of the owners in regard to advertising. Real horticulturists have no need for showmanship; their reputations suffice, so don't be swayed by dazzling claims or glamorous catalogs.

To sum up: purchase trees, shrubs and annuals locally whenever possible, especially when instant gratification is desired (meaning plants that have reached their ultimate height or are close to it). For anything else, depend on mail-order houses.

35. PLANT SOURCES

When it comes to annuals and mature shrubs and trees, it's wise to buy locally. You can actually *see* what you're getting, especially if you want quick results—which is often the case with city gardeners, especially terrace owners. When all you're shopping for is one tree and three or four shrubs, you don't want to have to wait five years before they begin to fill the spaces allocated to them. Local nurseries, catering to city gardeners, usually are smart enough to stock up on those plants that can take city pollution, excessive heat and high winds. But don't depend entirely on it. Arm yourself with sufficient knowledge to *know* which plants are best for ground-level gardens and which ones tolerate a high-in-the-sky environment. That's the chief purpose of the charts in this book, so do study them carefully.

Once you have the basic background plants in your garden and the hard-working annuals are contributing the needed color, you may begin to yearn for some of the more out-of-the-ordinary plants that add character and quality to a garden. Understandably, this can only be feasible if you have the space, but even a tiny corner somewhere can be sufficient to plant one unusual specimen. You may be lucky enough to live within a few hours' driving distance of a fine, well-stocked nursery. If not, you have a large number of excellent mail-order nurseries to choose from. Send for their catalogs, and a whole new world will open up to you. You may be inspired to try out new ideas you never thought possible before because you couldn't obtain the plant material, such as a small rock garden in a sunny spot or a few water plants in a tiny pool. Read these catalogs carefully, keeping in mind that as a city dweller you are bound by certain limitations. But there's such a wide range of plants available that you can be sure there will be something pretty special and beautiful for your garden. Don't be afraid to write to the nurseries and tell them about your own problems. They depend on repeat business and satisfied customers, so you can be sure the nurserymen will not recommend unsuitable plants. Culture requirements are included in the shipment, which is sent to you at just the proper time of the year for planting. So go to it and have fun!

Mail-Order Nurseries For General Plant Material

W. Atlee Burpee Co., 300 Park Avenue, Warminster, Pa. 18974

Kelly Bros. Nurseries, Dansville, N.Y. 14437

George W. Park Seed Co., Inc., Greenwood, S.C. 29647

Spring Hill Nurseries, Tipp City, Ohio 45336

Stern's Nurseries, Geneva, N.Y. 14456 (catalog 50¢)

White Flower Farm, Litchfield, Conn. 06759 (catalog $3 but worth it)

Specialized Mail-Order Nurseries

Azaleas, rhododendrons

Warren Baldsiefen, Box 88, Bellvale, N.Y. 10912 (catalog $2)

The Bovees Nursery, 1737 S.W. Coronado Street, Portland, Oreg. 97219 (catalog 25¢)

Orinda Nursery, Bridgeville, Del. 19933 (catalog 50¢)

Bamboo

Pacific Bamb-o Gardens, Box 16145, San Diego, Calif. 92116 (catalog 40¢)

Bulbs (also corms and tubers)

Antonelli Brothers, 2545 Capitola Road, Santa Cruz, Calif. 95060

P. de Jager & Sons, South Hamilton, Mass. 01982

International Growers Exchange, Box 397, Farmington, Mich. 48024 (catalog $2)

John Scheepers, Inc., 63 Wall Street, New York, N.Y. 10005

Van Bourgondien Bros., Box A, Babylon, N.Y. 11702

Vetterle Begonia Gardens, Box 1246, Watsonville, Calif. 95076

Chrysanthemums

Star Mums, West Grove, Pa. 19390

Clematis

D. S. George Nurseries, 2491 Benfield Road, Fairport, N.Y. 14450 (catalog 10¢)

Conifers (for rarities)

Fred W. Gergman, Raraflora, 1196 Stump Road, Feasterville, Pa. 19047

Joel W. Spingarn, 1535 Forest Avenue, Baldwin, N.Y. 11510 (catalog 50¢)

Dahlias

Douglas Dahlias, Route 1, Box 91, Myrtle Creek, Oreg. 97457

Ruschmoor Dahlia Gardens, Box 236, Rockville Centre, N.Y. 11571

Ferns and wildflowers

Alpines West Gardens, Route 2, Box 259, Spokane, Wash. 99207 (catalog 50¢)

Arthur Eames Allgrove, North Wilmington, Mass. 01887 (catalog 50¢)

Putney Nursery, Putney, Vt. 05346

The Wild Garden, 8243 N.E. 119th, Kirkland, Wash. 98033 (catalog $1)

Heaths, heathers

Sylvan Nursery, 1028 Horseneck Road, South Westport, Mass. 02790

Hemerocallis

Starmont Daylilies, 16415 Shady Grove Road, Gaithersburg, Md. 20760

Herbs

Caprilands Herb Farm, Silver Street, Coventry, Conn. 06238

Hilltop Herb Farm, Box 866, Cleveland, Tex. 77327 (catalog 35¢)

Iris

Gable Iris Gardens, 2443 38th Avenue South, Minneapolis, Minn. 55406

Summerlong Iris Gardens, R.D. 2, Box 163, Perrysville, Ohio 44864

Rock garden plants

Gardens of the Blue Ridge, Ashford, McDowell County, N.C. 28603 (also lots of rare wild flowers and other plants)

Roses

Jackson & Perkins Co., Medford, Oreg. 97501

Mini-Roses, Box 4255, Station A, Dallas, Tex. 75208

Nor'east Miniature Roses, 58 Hammond Street, Rowley, Mass. 01969

Sedums and sempervivums

Oakhill Gardens, Route 3, Box 87, Dallas, Oreg. 97338

Trees and shrubs (for rarities)

    Brimfield Gardens Nursery, 245 Brimfield Road, Wethersfield, Conn. 06109 (catalog $1)

    Dauber's Nurseries, Box 1746, York, Pa. 17405

    Gossler Farms Nursery, 1200 Weaver Road, Springfield, Oreg. 97477 (catalog 25¢)

Water lilies

    Three Springs Fisheries, Lilypons, Md. 21717 (catalog 50¢)

    Van Ness Water Gardens, 2460 North Euclid Avenue, Upland, Calif. 91786 (catalog 50¢)

Miscellaneous

    For decorative garden pools of assorted shapes and sizes, as well as accessories (including tiny bridges and fiber glass rocks), send to Hermitage Gardens, P.O. Box 361, Route 5, Canastota, N.Y. 13032, for their catalog. Paradise Gardens, Bedford and May Streets, Whitman, Mass. 02382, is also a source for these.

    For information and sources of distribution regarding Featherock (very lightweight stones of volcanic origin) used in naturalistic designs around pools or for mini-scaled Oriental gardens, write to Featherock, Inc., 2890 Empire Street, P.O. Box 6190, Burbank, Calif. 91510. However, you may be able to obtain this locally or through mail-order houses, as this product is now very popular.

    If you're looking for something extra-special in a garden ornament to be used as a focal point, of top quality in both workmanship and design, send for the catalogs of the following firms. Both long-established and of deserved eminence in the field, they are Erkins Studios, 8 West 40th Street, New York, N.Y. 10018 and Florentine Craftsmen, 650 First Avenue, New York, N.Y. 10016.

Bibliography

It may take a long time, but once he has become hooked by gardening, the city gardener cannot be surpassed for enthusiasm and dedication to his hobby. Maybe it's because space is so limited, a constant challenge to one's skill to make the most of it; or perhaps it's because of the many urban problems that must be surmounted. Probably it's because there is so little greenery in the midst of skyscrapers and concrete that every patch of garden becomes precious, and the tensions that go with living in the fast tempo are somewhat eased by working among plants and attending to their needs.

Most cliff dwellers are satisfied with their gardens if they look green and healthy; this in itself is an achievement! But there are other people who want to increase their knowledge of gardening so that it not only becomes a pleasurable hobby, but also helps them to create a garden that is uniquely their own, growing plants that are more challenging and displaying them in imaginative ways.

Knowledge and experience must go hand in hand in order to achieve success, whatever the endeavor. For the gardener, it means *doing*: cultivating the soil, growing plants, observing them, learning from the successes and the failures. But it also means *knowledge*, that which is available to him through books written by experts in the field, who have devoted many years to horticulture and to keeping up with the latest developments. Armed with what he has read, the gardener can go out in his garden and put it into practice. The experts are by no means *always* right. Fickle Nature sees that there are enough exceptions to the rules to remind us to be humble when dealing with her, but the average gardener has a greater chance of success if he takes advantage of the accumulated knowledge of professionals, plus his own hard-achieved experience.

A lengthy list of gardening books can be confusing, especially to the beginner gardener. I have limited mine to those categories of gardening that are of most interest to the city dweller. There are so many periodicals that I have not attempted to list them. Some are of a general nature; others are regional or specialize in only one plant category. A visit to your local library will give you an idea of what is available and what may appeal to you. There is a newsletter–digest publication–however, that is exceptionally well put together and manages to keep the gardener up-to-date on the latest happenings without going into lengthy essays about it. It's to the point and informative. While the subject matter is general, there is enough in it that would be useful to the dedicated city gardener. It's sold only by subscription, $10 per year: *The Avant Gardener*, Box 489, New York, N.Y. 10028.

General Books
(One all-around reference book is a must)
America's Garden Book, James and Louise Bush-Brown (Scribners, $12.50).
Taylor's Encyclopedia of Gardening, Norman Taylor (Houghton Mifflin, $17.50).
Wyman's Gardening Encyclopedia, Donald Wyman (Macmillan, $17.50).

Trees, Shrubs, Ground Covers, Vines
The Complete Book of Ground Covers, Robert E. Atkinson (McKay, $7.95).
Dwarf Shrubs, Donald Wyman (Macmillan, $7.95).
The Guide to Garden Shrubs and Trees, Norman Taylor (Houghton Mifflin, $9.95).
Rhododendrons and Azaleas, Clement Gray Bowers (Macmillan, $15.95).

Shrubs and Vines for American Gardens, Donald Wyman (Macmillan, $14.95).

Vegetables—Herbs

Gardening with Herbs, Helen Morgenthau Fox (Dover, $2.50 paperback).

The Green Thumb Book of Fruit and Vegetable Gardening, George Abraham (Prentice-Hall, $7.95).

Vegetables and Fruits, James Underwood Crockett (Time-Life Books, $7.95).

Vegetables for Today's Gardens, R. Milton Carleton (Wilshire Book, North Hollywood, Calif., $2.00).

Annuals, Perennials, Bulbs

Annuals, James Underwood Crockett (Time-Life Books, $7.95).

Ferns to Know and Grow, F. Gordon Foster (Hawthorn, $7.95).

Handbook of Wild Flower Cultivation, Kathryn S. Taylor and Stephen B. Hamblin (Macmillan, $7.95).

Hardy Garden Bulbs, Gertrude S. Wister (Dutton, $5.95).

Specialized Books

Container Gardening Outdoors, George Taloumis (Simon & Schuster, $7.95).

Diseases and Pests of Ornamental Plants, P. P. Pirone (Ronald, $13.50).

Growing Ornamentals in Urban Gardens, Henry M. Cathey (Home & Garden Bulletin No. 188, Superintendent of Documents, Government Printing Office, Washington, D.C. 20404, 15¢).

Hanging Gardens: Basket Plants Indoors and Out, Jack Kramer (Scribners, $6.95; $4.95 paperback).

The Japanese Art of Miniature Trees and Landscapes, Yuji Yoshimura and G. M. Halford (Tuttle, $10.95 paperback).

Plant Disease Handbook, Cynthia Westcott (Van Nostrand-Reinhold, $19.95).

The Pruning Handbook, Roy Hudson (Prentice-Hall, $2.95 paperback).

Rock Gardening, H. Lincoln Foster (Houghton Mifflin, $7.00).
Water Gardening, Jack Kramer (Scribners, $6.95; $3.95 paperback).

Of special note: There are two sources of excellent handbooks which are not only reasonably priced but packed full of invaluable information, written in a no-nonsense, easy-to-understand manner—no small feat in the horticultural field! One is the Brooklyn Botanic Garden (1000 Washington Avenue, Brooklyn, N.Y. 11225), whose handbooks cover a wide range of topics, such as "Summer Flowers for Continuing Bloom," "Gardening in the Shade," "Rock Gardens," "Mulches," etc. They cost $1 to $1.50 each. Send for their list of handbooks.

The other source is the Lane Book Company, Menlo Park, Calif. 94025, whose series of Sunset Gardening Books covers subjects such as "Succulents and Cactus," "Herbs," "Vegetable Gardening," "Outdoor Lighting," "Garden Art and Decorations," etc. Most of the handbooks cost $1.95. They're available in large garden supply centers. The one on pruning is one of the best guides on that subject that I've come across, in both illustrations and text.

Index